**Literature
in
Exile**

Literature
in
Exile

Edited by John Glad

Duke University Press

Durham and London

1990

I wish to express my special gratitude to
Susan Ashe, Norman Di Giovanni, and Aleksey Gibson
for the invaluable assistance they rendered in
preparing this book.

Permission to reprint the following articles is
gratefully acknowledged:
Nuruddin Farah: "In Praise of Exile," *Third World
Affairs of 1988, Third World Quarterly.* Reprinted
with permission from Third World Foundation for
Social and Economic Studies.
Joseph Brodsky: "The Condition We Call Exile."
Copyright © 1987 by Joseph Brodsky. Reprinted by
permission of Farrar, Straus and Giroux, Inc.

Contents

Preface   vii

The Philosophical Significance of Exile, William Gass   1
Discussion: Nuruddin Farah, Jan Vladislav, Jorge Edwards

Aquae et ignis interdictio, Yury Miloslavsky   8

Exile, Responsibility, Destiny, Jan Vladislav   14
Discussion: Antonin Liehm, William Gass, Virgil Tanase,
Nuruddin Farah, Jan Vladislav, Jirí Gruša

The Portable Ghetto, Jirí Gruša   28

The Invisible Exile, Guillermo Cabrera Infante   34
Discussion: William Gass

Exile Is Rebellion, Horst Bienek   41
Discussion: Virgil Tanase, Libuše Moníková, Jan Vladislav

Thirteen Studies on Exile, Edward Limonov   49
Discussion: Horst Bienek

Words of Exile, Nedim Gürsel   59
Discussion: Richard Kim, Nuruddin Farah

In Praise of Exile, Nuruddin Farah   64
Discussion: Jan Novak, William Gass, Jorge Edwards,
Nedim Gürsel, Antonin Liehm, Richard Kim, Horst Bienek,
Jaroslav Vejvoda

The Swelling Exodus, Jaroslav Vejvoda 78
Discussion: Edward Limonov, Libuše Moníková,
Virgil Tanase, Yury Miloslavsky, Dennis Brutus,
Anton Shammas, Nedim Gürsel

Exile from a Democracy, Anton Shammas 84
Discussion: Guillermo Cabrera Infante, Lev Kopelev,
Vladimir Voinovich, Horst Bienek, Edward Limonov, William Gass,
Georgy Vladimov, Sergei Dovlatov, Jirí Gruša, Richard Kim

The Condition We Call "Exile", Joseph Brodsky 100
Discussion: Jirí Gruša, Nedim Gürsel, Edward Limonov,
Raissa Orlova, Antonin Liehm, Libuše Moníková, Jan Vladislav,
Jan Novak, Yury Miloslavsky, Anton Shammas, Richard Kim,
Nuruddin Farah, Lev Kopelev, Adam Zagajewski

The Exile as Writer: A Conversation about Sorrow
and Joy, Wojciech Karpinski 131

An Exercise in Futility: The Case of Andrei Kurbsky,
Tomas Venclova 139

Report of a New Arrival, Yuri Druzhnikov 149
Introduced by Lev Kopelev   Discussion: Dennis Brutus,
Nuruddin Farah, Jaroslav Vejvoda

Glossary of Names 155
Notes on Contributors 162

Preface

Not so long ago politicians preferred to imprison or kill writers who made them feel uncomfortable. Nowadays, such writers find themselves rushed off to the airport, where they're usually told to pay for their own tickets. And then they're gone—as good as dead and with no claim even to a pension. The politicians have made a gesture that is both "humane" and convenient. Of course, writers are a noisy lot and are sure to try to keep on making trouble, but the politicians know they're just "cadavers on leave" (Goebbels's words about exiled German writers). And if they get too troublesome, someone can always be hired to persuade them by means of a pickax (Stalin's solution for Trotsky), or an order can be placed to the Bulgarian umbrella factory for a few "special models." Despite Victor Hugo's claim that "exile is life," politicians really prefer Ovid: "Exile is death."

Later, when passions cool down, there may even follow a sort of life after death. Even before Hungary took up the banner of *glasnost*, some Hungarian exiles were able to make accommodations with the authorities back home and continued to publish in Hungary. The Hungarian editor Gyula Borbándi even returned to Hungary—while continuing to edit an émigré journal abroad.

From the point of view of the writer, however, exile is at best a mixed bag. The writer abroad encounters obstacles far greater than those in the path of the stay-at-home. First of all, his chief tool—

language—is often useless. Furthermore, his former way of life—national history, food, television shows, road signs, etc., etc.—is irrelevant (and perhaps even uninteresting) in the new context. As a result, literature ceases to be a meaningful source of income for the overwhelming majority of writers in exile. Many end up subsidizing publication of their books, transforming their profession into a hobby. This is not to denigrate the word "hobby," but how do you pay the rent?

For better or worse, literature has been "professionalized" for a long time. If people used to tell *each other* stories to pass the evenings, we now have professional writers and professional readers—critics, professors. This (by definition) unnatural state of affairs requires that the artistic system compete within an ever-expanding spectrum of nonliterary pastimes. But exiles are a stubborn bunch; if they weren't, most of them would probably have stayed at home. They refuse to acknowledge a decline in their profession and have even made exile literature into a growth industry—at least as judged by a head count of authors. Nor are their efforts limited to "testimony." The very trauma of exile is an artistic stimulus. People who might never have taken up the pen under normal circumstances react to exile with a burst of creativity.

This book is based on a conference of writers in exile, held on December 2–5, 1987, in Vienna by the Wheatland Foundation of New York. The conference was organized by Rose Marie Morse, Executive Director of the Wheatland Foundation, and Anita Birchenall, its Executive Secretary, and it was sponsored by Saul and Gayfryd Steinberg of New York. The work on the book, based on the transcripts and papers submitted to the conference, was made possible in part through a grant from the National Endowment for the Humanities, an independent federal agency. The working languages of the conference were English, French, German, and Russian.

The writers' discussions at the conference clearly revealed that the exile experience is far from uniform. From the point of view of the Turkish writer in France, the "exile" status of an Argentine writer in Venezuela may well be questionable. And if we include here the Moroccan French writer or the Anatolian Greek forced to return to their respective countries of ethnic origin, the term "exile" is being stretched very far indeed. Ultimately, exile is a political rather than an artistic concept. Exile is when you can't go back. James Baldwin, a black American writer who spent most of his time in France, had this in mind when he said: "I don't consider myself an exile; I don't consider myself an expatriate. I guess I'm a sort of commuter." Then there is Hemingway; when he returned to the United States, did he "repatriate"? Was Gertrude Stein an "exile"? Now that the winds of *glasnost* and *perestroika* have blown across the Soviet Union and many exiled Russian writers obviously could return home if they wanted to, should they continue to consider themselves "banished"?

The phrase "literature in exile" has a ring of finality about it. Either you are or are not a "writer in exile." In point of fact, literary creation outside the boundaries of one's native land is a stone of many facets, only one of which is exile. I suggest here a multidimensional model of this process.

First of all, we could classify the author according to the circumstances under which he finds himself or herself abroad. Does he view his sojourn as temporary? Or is he an "expatriate"—one who regards his new address as his "current primary" residence, but who returns home from time to time? Then again he may be an "internal émigré"? (Both the Nazi and Soviet governments liked this term). Such a writer does not leave, but might like to. At the very least, foreign grass strikes him as being a lot greener than homegrown sod. Next in this gradation is the "involuntary émigré," who makes the decision to leave under coercion. Finally we have the true "exile," who is transported abroad against his will and is not permitted to return even for a visit. Like most taxonomies, this one too has its joker—second- and third-generation émigré writers. Where do they fit?

Dimension no. 2 in this model has to do with production—the place of publication of the work. Did it take place in the writer's home country (legally or clandestinely), or did it roll off a foreign press?

Production is followed by marketing, bringing us to dimension no. 3: who are the intended *primary* readers—those "back home"? In such cases the book might be legally distributed or smuggled into the country. If the intended readers reside outside the writer's country of origin, are they other émigrés or foreigners?

Dimension no. 4: of what magnitude are the differences in the way of life of the host country from that of the country of origin—roughly comparable (Germany to Scandinavia), significantly different (Hungary to Austria), radically different (USSR to U.S.A.), or overwhelmingly different (Somalia to France; for example, the case of Nurrudin Farah, who participated in the Wheatland Conference)?

Dimension no. 5: the language of the host country. Is it the same as that of the author's country of origin? If it is different, would he rather "fight than switch"?

Dimension no. 6 is the most emotional one—repatriation. If the option is available, does the writer accept or reject it? If he rejects it, does the long arm of native justice reach out for him anyway, as in the case of Ezra Pound? If he can't go home, does he even want to? Or perhaps he is unsure about his options (as in the case of Russian writers now, in the era of *glasnost* and *perestroika*)?

One of the central questions of literature in exile is that of literary tradition. Does the exiled writer attempt to fit into the tradition of the country which received him, or does he cling to his native roots, writing chiefly for "the folks back home?" For the most part, the internationalists are the exception.

In theory, at least, there exists a third option: that of a distinct émigré tradition, separate from that of the country of origin. Russian émigré literature, for example, has a tradition which goes back some four and one quarter centuries. In the twentieth century alone, five distinct groups have left Russia: the peasants at the turn of the century who left for North America in search of employment; the Jews, who continued their earlier flight from the pogroms; the revolutionaries, some of whom returned to seize power in Russia and create the Soviet state; the "First Wave" (following the Civil War); the "Second Wave" (World War II); and the "Third Wave" (beginning in the early seventies). Thus there has been a continuous émigré presence outside of Russia during the twentieth century, but each of these groups has maintained itself largely as a first-generation entity. The latest arrivals were educated and artistically formed without any real influence from earlier groups. Contiguity and continuity do not necessarily coincide; a row of pencils placed end to end does not fuse into a totality. The maintenance of a separate, viable tradition has shown itself to be a will-o'-the-wisp for Russian émigré letters.

Latin American literature, which is sometimes said to have its capital in Madrid, could serve as a model of an "émigré" tradition (for that matter, so could literature in Canada and the United States), and by that standard the theoretically possible separate émigré tradition remains a theory. A possible candidate is Jewish literature—an émigré tradition which for centuries was without a homeland. Perhaps an even better model would be Chinese émigré culture—a tradition which has existed for centuries, resisting assimilation.

The question of language often serves as a watershed. When Nabokov switched from Russian to English, the Russian émigré literary historian Gleb Struve declared that Nabokov had "ceased to be a Russian writer." But does that mean that Beckett has become a French writer? Was Conrad no longer a Pole?

Émigré letters definitely have one thing in common with non-émigré letters: it is not the creative writers who explicate the literary work to the public, but critics and literary historians, who take for granted that a sparrow is the last creature to ask about the principles of aerodynamics and that writers are an instinctual lot, totally divorced from theory.

The Wheatland Conference gave writers in exile an opportunity to discuss what is important to them. Here, in a nutshell, is what they wanted to talk about:

(a) History. Has the role and meaning of exile changed? Whom do the exiled writers regard as their predecessors?

(b) Leaving. Do writers leave their native countries out of admiration for a different country or culture, or are they usually driven out by negative pressures? Once they've left, what are their obligations to and relationships with colleagues and readers back home?

(c) Politics. What role can the émigré play? Is the so-called "internal émigré" an exile? What are the taboos of the new society?

(d) Literary tradition. Is the exiled writer primarily concerned with preserving his national tradition or with opening up to new influences? What are the favorite topics of the exiled writer? Is he part of the avant-garde of an incipient "world literature"?

(e) Language. Does living abroad undermine or, at the very least, influence the writer's language? Can the writer change languages? If he does so, is this an enrichment or an impoverishment? If the writer translates his own book, does he create a new work?

(f) The émigré condition. How does the new society treat the émigré? What is his role in this new society? Is the condition of exile a curse or a blessing? How different is the situation of the émigré who only began to write once he was abroad from that of the writer who had already established his literary credentials at home? Should the émigré writer strive toward literary/social integration in the new community? What is the nature of a creative process doomed to be ignored, given the conditions of exile? What sort of ego must an author have to accept such odds?

(g) Commonalities and differences. What do exiled writers have in common, regardless of country of origin, and what are the factors that differ from one national group to another? Are there national literary traditions which exercise a greater influence on the exiled writer than do others?

(h) Money.

Strangely (but not surprisingly) the writers seemed to be uninterested in the adequacy or inadequacy of their translators, perhaps because they were still oriented toward the audience "back home." Unlike Latin American authors, who can move from one Spanish-speaking country to another without switching languages, most exile writers not only have to reach a new primary audience, they must do so in a new language. Thus the émigré or exiled writer is far more dependent on the translator than is the non-émigré, who can look upon royalties from translated works as icing on the cake.

Not long ago, I asked a certain émigré author (who shall remain anonymous) about a translation of one of his novels. He rummaged around his bookshelves and finally came up with the edition—still shrink-wrapped. He had never bothered even to open the book. Another émigré writer once heaped the ultimate abuse on an unloved colleague: he dismissed him as a "translator from the German."

Partly as a result of this attitude, and even more as a consequence of low pay, many translators are recruited from the ranks of the untalented, and their slipshod work is—in a sad way—a fitting repayment for this state of affairs. The upshot of all this, of course, is that exiled writers who were popular at home are often unable to find a reading public in their new environment.

Another topic to receive only scant attention was the perhaps ultimate question, that of repatriation. In the early stages of emigration the question of return is foremost (favorite fantasy: conquering hero on a white steed), but as time passes the links with those back home weaken and the desire to return is replaced by a desire to pay a visit (this time the fantasy is a cozy pied-à-terre in Leningrad, Buenos

Aires, Shanghai . . .). Nevertheless, some writers go still further in the rejection of that which they left behind: Thomas Mann, who declared that any book published between 1934 and 1945 was "smeared with blood and shame," announced after the war that even a visit to Germany would be a disorienting and unpleasant experience.

Frank Thiess, a German writer who did not emigrate, responded: "Truly, it is not an ocean that lies between him [Mann] and us, but an abyss. Neither mountain ranges, nor languages, nor even the hatred of war . . . can separate people as effectively as the difference between those who have acquired knowledge through suffering and those who fall into ignorance in the protection of fame and 'honorary degrees.' "

In short, the meeting of German writers was a story of love and separation, of recriminations and explanations, of rejection and—ultimately—reconciliation. It was not the first such love story gone awry, and it most certainly will not be the last.

So what, ultimately, is it like to be an émigré? Boris Khazanov, a recent émigré from the USSR, summed it up:

> Here [in West Germany] only the yellow stubble in the harvested fields reminds you of Russia. And the thought crosses my mind: what if nothing had ever happened, if there had never been an escape, if I had just been brought here in my sleep: I see myself waking up and standing at the edge of a field and I wonder if I would realize that all around me lay a different country? What would signal to me of the change? Really, what is different? The grass is the same, and the roadside nettles and wild flowers haven't changed. It's like a game in which you have to guess the meaning of a text. Some of the letters are the same, and they form words. But the whole thing is void of meaning; it's a different language. Even the sky, if you look at it long enough, has a slightly different appearance—as if the gases comprising it were different here. An old man strolls in my direction talking to his dog in so alien a tongue you might imagine his vocal cords were constructed differently from mine. The tall-trunked, elegant, sunlit forest is not at all like our forests; you can ride though it on a bicycle, imagining yourself to be a sort of Siegfried. There is nothing left of the forest games we played back home, and a new sensation crowds out the old—a feeling of loneliness and freedom.

John Glad

**Literature
in
Exile**

Horst Bienek

Joseph Brodsky

Guillermo Cabrera Infante

Yuri Druzhnikov

Nuruddin Farah

William Gass

John Glad

Jiri Gruša

Nedim Gürsel

Wojciech Karpinski

Edward Limonov

Yury Miloslavsky

Anton Shammas

Jaroslav Vejvoda

Tomas Venclova

Jan Vladislav

William Gass

The Philosophical
Significance of Exile

———

I should like to welcome
you all to the second Congress of Vienna. This second congress
differs from the first in a few essentials, of course: we are not heads of
state, and we have not gathered here to carve up a continent, but only
to analyze a concept and describe a condition, or to investigate many
concepts and outline many conditions.

As we do so, we shall be pulled in two directions: on the one
hand, toward the engrossing immediate past and all of those things
which make up the concrete details of émigré or exile life; on the
other, toward the equally strong enticements of ideas and the lure of
ideology for the implications of thought. Somehow we must strike a
profitable balance between our rationalist and empirical impulses.

For many Americans the idea of exile must be a highly romantic
one, consisting principally of poets in Paris passing their time in
cafés and having their saucers counted. As the reality of exile itself
becomes customary and recedes into the past, these writers often
become as anecdotal as war is for its soldiers.

After Socrates was found guilty by an Athenian court, he was
lodged rather lightly in prison to wait for the end of an important
festival, when it was expected that he would spare the state the guilt
of his death by committing suicide. His friends came to him and
urged him to escape. The guards could be easily bribed.

Neither his friends nor his enemies were eager to endure Socrates the martyr. Dead, he would be as much trouble as he had been alive. So Socrates was offered exile as an alternative. What did this mean to him?

We all know that Socrates chose the hemlock. He was old; his work was done; he had a nag for a wife and a kid with a small goat's future. Death was nothing but dreamless sleep, he said, and even if there were another life, he could then continue his questions and his conversations there, making a veritable hell of an otherwise vapid and shadowy underworld. But his real reason was that he considered exile an amputation of self. Socrates was essentially an Athenian, and to be an Athenian was to continue to practice what he took to be his proper role in the city, that of the gadfly. Socrates did not believe a mute, inglorious Socrates was possible, but his choice depended on a conception of the relation between the citizen and the city (we would now say between the individual and the state), which has almost entirely disappeared in our time.

That conception has been replaced by two others, quite opposed to one another. The first might be called the utilitarian view: that society is, or ought to be, a source of human happiness, an instrument of the citizen's well-being. And if society does not perform its function well, the citizen has the right to seek another, as he might choose a screwier screwdriver, or divorce an unfulfilling spouse. When things go wrong, it is the state which is sent into exile. Perhaps that is too strongly put, because the instrumental relation is weak and does not deserve the term "exile."

Then we have the so-called collective view: the individual serves society, has a place and station, function and fitting within it; the players come and go, but the Notre Dame football team carries on forever. Each of us occupies a position in the collective, and if we cannot correctly carry out the tasks that define our nature, we are replaced by someone who will. When a player graduates, or is sent to the bench, or is traded to another team, he is not sent into exile, because for his original team he no longer exists. Only he, banished as he is, traded unkindly to another team, may feel exiled. That is because in his own eyes he has come apart; he needed that role in society to be what he was; now he no longer has that role, and shortly he will realize that without an essence he is nothing; he is naught.

Socrates, however, felt that the city was like his right arm, an important part of himself. Not his entire body and soul, surely, but a vital element. His arm served him, indeed as a hammer or a screw-driver might, but when his arm became weak, he did not, could not, replace it. Instead he tended it; he nursed it; he sought its health and hoped for its goodwill.

According to one view then, to take the family as the model, I marry because I hope it will cure my nervous afflictions, because it will elevate me in society, because my intended spouse is rich, and so on. I expect the family to help me be happy. From the other point of view, the family is a set of functions—husband, mother, daughter; the family endures, even if wives are run through faster than they run through their own hose. According to this view you do not divorce your husband; you simply replace him with a man who will do a better job.

Finally, there is Socrates's view: if some member of the family is weak and inadequate, that member must be looked after, not abandoned, just as you would not abandon your physiognomy, although in these days of plastic surgery that is increasingly possible. You would not leave a limb behind, unless you were a rat in a trap, unless your leg were gangrenous, unless it threatened the rest of you with death.

Exile, in this ancient sense, is a severing of blood; it is a loss of family ties, of clan identity, of cultural definition. You are not exiled from your work if you have simply lost a job when another job will do as well. Socrates would not only have been deprived of his position in the polis, he would have been deprived of that philosophical activity which was his life.

The lost limb yearns to rejoin its body; the body, however it pretends to have adjusted to its loss by calling it necessary, imagines that limb is still in place, and puts the old pain back in the empty air, where the flesh once was.

Personally, I would not allow my family to define me, and I will not allow the state to do it either. At any rate, the political aspects of my society, and many of the social ones as well, do not permit an artist that kind of close allegiance. Socrates could embrace a society that had condemned him because it was still a part of his soul's anatomy. But if the state were to cast me out as an undesirable, it would be (as I presently pretend, at any rate) like being thrown from a horse in some old movie. High-ho Honda, I would then say instead, and drive away.

But suppose I were deprived of my tongue, my power of speech, my language. He who steals my comforts steals trash (and probably does me a favor), but whoever takes even a sliver from my essential self, however unsocial that self has been forced to become, takes a sliver from the head and impales it in the heart.

Birth is your first experience of exile, the Greeks maintained. That's why a child bellows when it is born: it discovers into what life it has been thrust. The second exile is never really to belong, to have quit before you were fired. And the third exile is to forget the enormity of your loss.

I hope these remarks will at least put something in front of us for discussion, and if not these remarks, others which you may have considered, before coming, or at the moment. So now I wish simply to open the discussion.

Nuruddin Farah   In response to William Gass's remarks, I would like to talk very briefly about the metaphysical nature of exile, linking it to the philosophical one.

What is the topic of literature? It began with the expulsion of Adam from paradise. What, in fact, writers do is to play around either with the myth of creation or with the myth of return. And in between, in parentheses, there is that promise, the promise of return. While awaiting the return, we tell stories, create literature, recite poetry, remember the past, and experience the present. Basically, we writers are telling the story of that return—either in the form of a New Testament or an Old Testament variation on the creation myth. It's a return to innocence, to childhood, to our sources. That's one aspect.

The other aspect lies in that particularly contentious power that has to do with speech. In the beginning was the Word, but the myth created by God is challenged by the author, who thinks of himself as a little god. The politician, who is a pedestrian in every sense of the term, would like to challenge the little god, that is, the writer.

Jan Vladislav   I am of Czech origin and I now live in France. I am, to tell the truth, a bit torn as to whether I should speak in German, which I speak in the streets of Vienna, or in English, which I speak with my American and English friends and others, or in French, which has become my second language after Czech, my mother tongue and the language of my poetry. This is one of the problems of exile: language—but which language? I should like to say in passing that this opportunity to use many languages, to speak and experience them, is one of the positive aspects of exile.

My main topic, however, is the very notion of exile. Is exile the same for all exiles? Was exile in antiquity the same thing as exile today, in modern society?

Did the problem and the concept of exile exist in the Middle Ages, for example? Did it exist for the common people, as well as for the musicians, the artists, and the painters of the seventeenth, eighteenth, and nineteenth centuries?

I happen to have read several books on eighteenth- and nineteenth-century music, and on Czech-speaking musicians educated in Bohemia and Moravia who heard music performed in their own country and then went to Vienna to study and work, or to Italy—to Venice, Naples, and Rome.

Some went to Paris. Rejcha, known in France as Recha, became a professor at the Conservatoire de Paris. A Czech, he taught French musicians such as Gounod, César Franck, and Berlioz. He became "Reicha," a member of the French Academy and a French citizen, and he was decorated with the Legion of Honor. Although he became French, he also remained Czech.

Others went to London. People went everywhere, and for them the problem of exile did not exist. They did not think of themselves as exiles, but felt, in some sense, at home everywhere.

Perhaps we should view the notion of exile as a legacy of eighteenth- and nineteenth-century nationalism. Borders were created, which then required passports. Exile, I believe, exists in numerous forms, although ultimately it is the basic condition of all men.

Jorge Edwards As we have been discussing the philosophical nature of exile, I would like to make some remarks about the changing historical nature of this condition, basing my comments on my own Chilean experience.

Chilean writers have always lived in an atmosphere of exile. Although our writers were not forced to leave, Chile took in many exiles, so we were always among exiles—Peruvian, Brazilian, Cuban, Argentine. This is part of Chilean literature. In the nineteenth century, for instance, many of the best Argentine writers participated very actively in Chilean life and in our universities.

At the same time, voluntary or self-imposed exile played an important part in Chilean writing. Every Chilean writer, artist, and intellectual felt it essential to travel to the centers of world culture. This was a Chilean obsession. One Chilean writer said that his epitaph should read: "He wanted to be a writer, but he became a Chilean writer."

Vicente Huidobro, one of our great poets, spent half his life in Paris, trying to become a French writer. When on one of his travels back to Chile he was asked by a journalist how it felt to be home, he replied (in French) that he felt *très bien*, because Chile was his second homeland. His first was France.

Most of these writers went through a curious evolution in their lives. Ultimately they were forced to adapt and resign themselves to being Chilean writers, and for the most part they returned, rather like elephants, to die at home.

Today, however, we have what for us is a new experience, and a hard and painful one—real exile, government imposed. This is an example of the changing historical nature of exile.

Chilean writers fought hard against it. We formed committees to facilitate the return of exiles to Chile. Our writers' union has a regulation dating back to 1938 or 1939, still in effect, that permits us to convene a congress of Chilean writers once a year. We used the regulation to organize such a congress, and we invited Chilean writers who were in exile. We went through all the red tape, and the government allowed some, but not all of them, to return. So we cancelled the congress in protest against banning those few who were not allowed in.

The problem, as you know, exists to this very day, although it has to be said that many of those writers have since been able to return.

Last year in West Berlin, while participating in a series of readings by Latin American writers, I had a curious experience. The readings were broken down in what was to me an odd, arbitrary, and even ignorant fashion. There was a reading entitled "Authors in Exile," and then another reading by people like me, who were simply defined as Chilean writers. In fact, just two weeks earlier I had seen one of those *autores in exilio* in a café in Santiago, where he was spending his holidays. So some of the writers in exile are exiles only according to the old definition—those who left Chile to make a literary career for themselves. However, some writers still cannot go back to Chile. [This was true at the time of the conference, but is no longer the case.—ed.]

Yury Miloslavsky

Aquae et ignis interdictio
(Deprived of Fire and Water)

———

In my language the word "ex-ile" has an air of carousal about it, suggesting blizzards and fate: "Proshchaite, farewell, we won't meet again." And so, not removing your Russian otter-fur cap, you bow down for the last time to the Russian soil, brush off the undercover agent escorting you, ascend the gangway with a dignified tread, and pause on the top step to cast a last backward glance. Droning mournfully, the contraption slips its mooring ropes, climbs shuddering into the air, and hurtles forward, vanishing into the irrevocable distance. The whole business is so marvelous that all I can do is point my ass at those suffering faces below and excrete, full pressure, in an acrid, yellow, wide-open sheaf, like the hoopoe bird defending its nest.

The once authoritative *Great Encyclopedia*, published in St. Petersburg at the end of the last century, defines "exile" as "the general condition of a person unable to live in his native land due to government decree, personal circumstances, or choice." The encyclopedia continues, "The Romans did not consider exile to be a punishment. . . . A person found guilty of a crime might move to another country. To prevent such an exile returning . . . a sentence of banishment, *interdictio aquae et ignis*, was decreed, i.e., he was to be cut off from the communal fire and water; if the exile nevertheless chose to return, it was lawful to kill him."

For citizens of many countries, the recent avalanche of progress has made exile the supreme reward, the lucrative lifelong business trip abroad to be sought at any cost. Tens of millions of people, it is claimed, dream of becoming exiles. At any event, tens of thousands of politicians, newsmen and government officials are nicely earning a living helping—or hindering—the fulfillment of this mass dream. These would-be exiles demand unimpeded, speedy and comfortable exile, and special conditions to aid their integration into the new countries. Those who make exile a profession are appointed to high-paying jobs as government experts on the problems of exile. They head the exile associations, contribute to the exile press, and receive decorations and pensions. The losers in this game (and there are not all that many) demand immediate government aid, threatening otherwise to return to the country that exiled them, thus adversely influencing potential exiles back home.

Like Laocoön, bound by a bull tapeworm, the exile is unable, even for a moment, to rid himself of curious incongruities: he exposes the atrocities of the exiling regime, pontificating about the serious and responsible work with which he was entrusted before his exile—by the same hideous regime. Ignorant of anything resembling a free election—even for a village mayor or a school janitor—the exile lambastes the society that has given him refuge for its inability to stand up for the defense of democratic freedoms. A partisan of strong rule, he nevertheless prefers to vegetate in countries ruled by governments of liberal persuasion, despite disorderliness, flourishing homosexuality and drug abuse (inspired, undoubtedly, by a network of totalitarian-communist agents).

Finally, the exile is extremely noisy.

It is a sunny day somewhere in Texas and two cowboys lounge in a small-town street, beside the hitching post. Suddenly, in a cloud of dust, straw and crushed chickens, a sinister rider gallops past. Gunshots roar out, and hoof beats thunder.

"Say, Harry, who could that be?" one of the cowboys drawls lazily.

"It's Joe; they'll never catch him."

"Oh!" exclaims the Simple Simon in awe. "But who's after him?"

"No one," comes the quiet reply.

Perhaps I'm unfair to this thick-set, corpulent, somewhat disturbed being who has grown into such an inveterate liar that one would be ill-advised to ask him the time of day. In the words of one Russian émigré, church historian Anton Kartashov, "his loss of conscience is incurable; he is warped, vain, and unhappy."

But that's the way we exiles are.

And that's the mildest thing that could be said of us, unless we mention the inevitable kicks in the ass—usually delivered with weary scorn: "Get out of here" or (sometimes with the vexed nervousness of a man trying to rid himself of a hated wife who doesn't want him to go to a bachelor's party): "Fuck off, you goddamned bitch!" Less frequent is the resounding, well-aimed kick: "Get lost, you slime, or you'll get what's coming to you." Having flitted off to a respectable distance, we snap back: "Just wait, you'll wish you hadn't been so shortsighted, but by then it'll be too late; I'll be back—in spirit, if not in the flesh."

It's clear, however, that no one will regret your loss, nor will there be anything, or anybody, to come back to, for the gap left by your departure soon begins to be filled with healing balm from within. To lay the blame for this process on the cruelty of the administration is ridiculous. Even more ridiculous are threats to reveal the whole truth and thereby show up the state in its true colors. Even if anyone other than the narrator (himself a great champion of truth) were to show interest in the exile's pitiful inside information, his intrinsic untrustworthiness and refusal to acknowledge defeat (and exile is just that—defeat, not victory!) would soon alienate even the sympathetic listener—assuming, naturally, that polling exiles is not part of his job.

Such was the death of Moscow-born Grigory Karpovich Kotoshikhin, a former junior official of the Russian Foreign Office. Treated unfairly at work, he defected to Sweden, where he wrote an excellent tract, known by scholars under the title *Russia during the Reign of Aleksei Mikhailovich*. In a drunken brawl Kotoshikhin stabbed and killed his landlord, who (I hope not without reason) suspected his tenant of a wanton liaison with the landlord's wife. "In accordance with the court verdict," writes the Swedish biographer and translator of Kotoshikhin, "he was forced to lay his head upon the block in the square outside Stockholm's southern gate. . . . Immediately afterwards his body was taken to Uppsala, where it was dissected by the learned Professor Magister Olaf Rudbeck. Strung onto copper and steel wire, his bones remain there till this day as a kind of monument."

Grigory Kotoshikhin deserves a novel—a novel which I ought to write—and his skeleton, set upon a suitable pedestal, could serve as a remarkable monument to all our exile lives. Several times I've thought of putting together a group of influential exiles to petition the Swedish government to hand over Kotoshikhin's bones, but certain differences of opinion in exile circles, provoked by the KGB, made me postpone this plan.

But it is time now to lay aside sarcastic witticisms and to forgive, or, at the very least, to feel shame. All that I've said so far has been what we call "journalism": the extension of one's limbs from the pulpit with the epileptoidal righteousness of a commissar worming his way into the very sanctuary. I must hurry, or even the tax-collectors and adulteresses will enter the Kingdom of Heaven before me. I want to find my place among them, and not be hopelessly late. It's almost fifteen years now since I left home, and I still seem to have learned nothing.

But what about the anguish of exile—the longing for the lost homeland's secondary sexual characteristics, once defined by that great Russian expert (more than that, our spokesman on exile affairs) Marina Tsvetaeva, as "a long since exposed nuisance"? This anguish is easy to summon up, especially if exile has turned out to be a financial success. In a decent restaurant you order a plate of ethnic hors d'oeuvres and a bottle of folkloric booze. In a bare fifteen minutes you imbibe the exquisite sadness of exile.

"*The wind does not carry here to me/*(emphasis mine) the wail of Russia's battle trumpets." These lines from Joseph Brodsky's ode contain in a condensed form an answer to the question: what does the writer do with exile? He demythologizes it, demotes it to the ranks, and puts it in its place—an honorable, lawful place, but no more than that. "Those sounds never reach me here." I know I'm here and I'm always ready to admit it. If desired, I can even provide the curious with a semiotic road map on which the symbols carry not the basic but only an auxiliary meaning, since I'm not trying to pass off as a map a landscape in oils on the theme "Parting."

"Let's assume the opposite," you say. "How does exile influence the writer who is cut off from the fire and water available to the rest of his compatriots?"

Courtesan-like as it may be in manner, the question nevertheless deserves an intelligible answer.

Speaking for myself, I don't regret a single day. Exile has permitted me to view my loss from different perspectives, to see it at an inaccessible distance and simultaneously to feel it in my gut. It has led me to take delight in the verbal crusts I would surely have scorned in more favorable circumstances. With only a mild degree of exaggeration, it could even be said that exile has put some sense into my head.

And then night falls, finding me midway between St. Elias Monastery and Bethlehem. I am lying in bed in a four-story apartment building shoddily constructed on rocky whitish ground. This land, called "Palestine," "the Holy Land," "the Promised Land," etc., was recently seized by one group of exiles from another group of exiles. The methods used were force and cunning. The palpably fresh evil has not yet had time to settle, to justify itself under the statute of limitations and become eligible for the amnesty of redemption which, in the opinion of the local philistines, is just a step away. So all of Palestine reeks of uncollected rubbish. The phosphorescent carcasses of dogs and cats crushed by automobiles lie scattered along the roads; when run over for a second time, they raise their heads, bare their teeth and hiss. Living here is both shameful and abominable, but I'm used to that.

Around two in the morning I am awakened—immediately, totally—by a piercing scream of fright. I don't know if it came from my own throat or from the street. I imagine the victim—prostrate, his balls exposed and vulnerable—and I sob: "Lord Jesus Christ, Son of God, have mercy on me a sinner!"

This night raid on the soul, this night vandalism, this night interrogation when they drag you down the stairs, face down, lasts until your tormentors come upon something silly, tongue-tied, drunk on cheap wine, filthy but invincible—invincible thanks to its stickiness, thickness, and ugliness. Let me call this spherical defense, which guards a delicate spiritual flesh, a sense of motherland—but not, of course, in the obscene imperial-patriotic sense. I am referring here to the tiny, thoroughly real and tangible area on which my feet stand (spreading out with age). At first they were wrapped in soiled blue-wool baby bootees, later in sandals, still later in black wrinkled shoes manufactured in Kharkov Shoe Factory No. 5, and finally in the extravagant French platform semiboots that were in style then and which my first wife bought me the day before our flight into exile.

Jan Vladislav

*Exile, Responsibility,
Destiny*

———

Man does not make the de-
cisions which most concern him. By the time he begins to be conscious of these facts, it is too late for him to change the date of his
birth or the place already designated by him and others as his country,
his *home*. Most people identify this home with their birthplace, but
home can also be found thousands of kilometers from one's native
soil. Some people traverse continents, only to discover, to their as-
tonishment, that they are *at home* simultaneously in many parts of
the globe, since our country, our home, refuge and anchorage, the center of gravity, which prevents us from falling back into nothingness, is
fixed above all in time.

This is not a new idea. Everyone knows that time—human
time—constitutes a sort of vertebral column to memory, and that
memory, in its turn, is the backbone of history, as much in the
individual as in the general sense. (Ultimately, man is at home at
those moments which his memory has led him to accept as his
country, his home, perhaps not without reflection, sometimes ad-
visedly, but always *after the event*.) This is why he can have many
homes, at once or successively, and it is why any country or countries
can exist, first and foremost, inside him. With some effort, or nostalgia, we can evoke our country's true geography. Slowly, but correctly,
we can redraw its faded contours. But it is impossible to return there
in reality. Not only has everything changed, but we ourselves are also

different, and above all, time has changed—ours, as well as everyone else's.

Our home is the place from which we originate, and toward which we turn to look from an ever-increasing distance. Our home is a point in time which we have lost, but can always rediscover, along with details which we would not even have noticed *then, on the spot.* For man, the immaterial, unreal time of mathematicians freezes and realizes itself in memory. This is not only a question of individual memory, for a man's home, fixed in time, is shaped not only by his own history, but also by the histories of those who surround him, by his family and tribe, and by the palpable history of tilled fields, of ancient villages and new cities, and above all by that changeable, unfathomable, mythic reservoir of his native language.

A man's native village can be engulfed by the waters of a dam, a city can be razed to the ground by bombs, a landscape can be rendered unrecognizable by the creative as well as the destructive activity of man. But one thing never changes. We never stop carrying within us this meeting place with ourselves, with all our successive and abandoned selves, this place of recognition, of acceptance or rejection of ourselves and the rest of the world. Perhaps that is the hell which each of us is said to carry in his heart. But if our hell is there, so too is our paradise.

Security, a firm ground on which to rest, if only for a moment, is what is essential to this paradise. Hell is perpetual transience. But these are only the right and wrong sides of human time. Every day, at every hour, its inflexible advance separates a man from his home. Exile is the prerogative of man: of all men, even if only a few—poets, artists, philosophers—know it, or have a premonition of it. The real choice is not between one's native land and exile. As Socrates knew, the real choice is between life and death. But neither is this altogether true, because, in fact, the alternative *does not exist*: there is no life without death, nor death without life. To accept the gift of life is also to accept death. To accept the home, a *place* which has merged with *time*, is to accept that one is forever leaving it.

The real question then is whether man can accept a life, and thus a death, that are not *his own*, whether he can accept a life that has been *imagined* for someone else and has been imposed on him by every possible means. The example of Socrates is revealing: a man of dignity inevitably wants to live his own life and die his own death. From the moment he begins to think, he strives to realize his own personality and that of the world around him. He must then, more or less consciously, make those decisions that fall within his own power, as opposed to those of birthplace and native country, which do not. Either he decides to lead his own life, or else he accepts an alien life. In the end, it does not matter *where*, in what part of the world. *To live one's own life* means to protect a home within oneself, an elusive yet real home. It means to provide a refuge for one's personal history, one's family traditions, one's language, one's ideas, one's *native land*. To live an alien life, even if only a few feet from his place of birth, is to lose all of this. To accept an alien life is to accept an alien death—and that is notably the lot of those forced into exile. The study of ancient or primitive cultures teaches us that rejection of a man from society is an age-old rite. It is a deprivation of that quintessential thing, a man's personality. The proscribed person ceases to be a *human being;* he is abandoned to die. His life is exposed to all sorts of dangers—to the whims of the gods, to nature, to wild animals and people. And he is abandoned to himself, for all this has occurred in accordance with the ways of that world—ways which he himself acknowledges with pleasure or displeasure.

In the modern world it is no longer possible to create outlaws in the same way. The state has at its disposal only one means of imposing a foreign existence on a man who wants to lead his own life: exile is a death penalty in effigy which aims at destroying everything that makes up a man's life, his history, his particular language, in brief, his *home*, and makes a foreigner of him everywhere. Only the man who is determined to refuse to live an alien, imaginary life is immunized against such a sentence, for it cannot reach his world. This path may lead to self-deception, suffering, and tragedy, but it will not destroy him. His native land, which has made him and which allows him to live his own life to the end, cannot be stolen from him. This native land, which a man cannot abandon and which even more cannot be stolen from him, is not a hope, but a certainty, on which each one of us can rely, wherever we may be, whether in our home town or ten thousand miles away.

Only in our own lives are we at home. The search for our own lives, and our resolve to live them, lend dignity to contemporary man. Every artist and thinker, for a long time now, has had the duty and the privilege of delineating contemporary man, of describing the way toward him, of throwing away those masks which he has accumulated knowingly or unknowingly, and of revealing his unique, authentic face. The duty and privilege continue, whether we are in our own country or elsewhere. At the worst we find ourselves in new situations, having to rethink our positions, our rights and obligations, our liberties and responsibilities.

In discussing human rights we should at the same time give thought to responsibility. Freedom and responsibility are two sides of the same coin. The greater the rights we demand on the freedom side, the greater are our duties on the responsibility side. These frequently forgotten axioms are applicable to everyone, but doubly so to people of learning, who, since ancient times, have occupied a special role in the community. Even if they do not strive directly for power in the community, in a sense they have it anyway. It is a particular kind of power. In general, it usually operates outside the established power structures and thus is feared, even though its resources are only words and ideas. Without doubt, the first representative of this independent power was Socrates. The Athenian philosopher, however, was not only an archetype of freedom but also a paragon of responsibility. His, of course, is the responsibility of the free individual who will heed the voice of conscience rather than someone else's orders. This is the sort of responsibility that refuses to defer to power, because its touchstone is truth.

To all intents and purposes this individual view of responsibility still applies, despite the thousand years of development that civilization has undergone. Any changes in modern times, that is, since the last century, may be attributable to the more generalized and acute nature of today's problems. Intellectuals have demanded increasing freedom of thought and creation, and indeed their disciplines—science, philosophy, art and literature—have gradually acquired an unprecedented degree of independence. On the other hand, society's demands on them have also grown, along with the resources which those in power are able to deploy, and which certain regimes do indeed deploy, not just to control the thinkers, but also to exploit them for their own ends. In short, while one side calls constantly for rights and freedom, the other side claims to have a monopoly on duty and responsibility.

But intellectuals and writers have as much regard for duty and responsibility as do their various critics and judges. The promptings of these mentors are superfluous to thinking men. It is not recognition of their responsibilities that is in question. What lies at the heart of these recurring controversies (as well as the occasional conflicts that flare up and seem to threaten both the future of literature and its creators) is the old Socratic question: *to what is this responsibility owed?*

Society, and a considerable number of writers themselves, tend to reply to this question with clichés about "service," particularly service to a "common cause." This can mean all sorts of things. In Czechoslovakia (but not only there) this cause was conceived in the last century primarily in national terms and frequently in the crudest sense of serving immediate needs that generally fell outside the scope of literature. In the name of such needs, a poet of the stature of Karel Hynek Mácha could be ridiculed, as could the first great Czech woman prose writer, Božena Němcová, whose works were reduced to the level of anecdotal tales and folklore.

Over the past hundred years a whole series of such political programs have come and gone in our country, all of which have stressed, more or less overtly and for every possible ideological or political motive, the paramount need for literature to *serve*. You can find this in any textbook. Although writers themselves have often helped to frame and advance these ideas, their aims and aspirations were introduced into literature from without, in disregard of the intrinsic meaning of literature.

In those periods when a whole array of different aims are able to coexist or compete freely, literature finds itself in no great danger. Writers not only have the opportunity to choose among alliances, but they can reject them all and seek out their own way, determining where their responsibility lies according to the dictates of their own conscience and without affecting their existence as writers. And even when conflicts arise with the powers that be, there are no serious consequences. The prosecution of Baudelaire's *Les fleurs du mal* not only served to publicize the book but encouraged the writer to rework it and improve it.

The situation is quite different in regimes which proclaim that a particular political program is universally applicable and binding. Even if they sincerely believe in the program, writers are sooner or later certain to find themselves in a state of insuperable inner conflict, which may lead to their outright rejection of the state's ideals. This will immediately bring them into conflict with the authorities, and face to face with all the consequences of such a conflict—from a rigorous censorship which forbids them publication, to the still-more-radical means which involves sending writers to forced-labor camps or to prison. The history of Czech and Slovak literature over the past forty years provides us with flagrant instances of this practice.

Our history has proven to be a series of different interpretations of the writer's role, as expressed by the authorities in speeches and at congresses. Among the pupils of Stalin and Zhdanov was the Bohemian Ladislav Štoll. His interpretation of the writer's responsibilities is nothing but a rehash of past formulas: the writer is always responsible to the proletariat, or more precisely, to its avant-garde—the Communist Party, the Politburo, the General Secretary. In a word, the principle criterion for evaluating the role of the Czechoslovak intellectual can be summed up in Joseph Stalin's term, "devotion." The chief error of several avant-garde Czech poets consisted in *not having found the words to glorify Stalin*, as Štoll (in a menacing tone) called upon them to do in his study *Thirty Years of Struggle for Czech Socialist Poetry*. In the 1950s, when this study appeared, it amounted to a written indictment of Czech literature.

Similarly tedious descriptions of the writer's role are to be found on the other side of the barricades; for example, in the article "Critical Remarks on the Civic Movement for Mutual Assistance," penned under a pseudonym by a sympathizer of "Charter 77" and published in 1982 in the exile magazine *Svědectvi* (Testimony). Its author, Martin Středa, devotes particular attention to the meaning and the mission of our nonofficial literature. Even though Středa does not share Štoll's political views, his concept of literature is every bit as utilitarian as that of this old-guard communist ideologue. Středa accuses nonofficial Czech literature of not being "sufficiently active," of "lacking an ethical rallying call," of not having "a communal program or even a concerted movement with a defined platform."

The cause of such a state of affairs he sees as the writers' defence of "professional privileges," particularly *freedom of expression*; "their greatest need and their greatest joy derives from the formulation of their own personal feelings." This last phrase says it all. According to Středa, the task, indeed the obligation, of the writer is to formulate ideas presented to him by someone else, someone more competent; in other words, the *ideologue*.

Party functionaries are not the only persons who would determine the duties of literature and the responsibilities of its authors, but such people can teach us nothing about the real meaning of the writer's work and his role in society. We should turn elsewhere; for example, to the philosopher Jan Patočka, who dealt with the question in his essay "Spisovatelova věc" (The Writer's Thing). The article was part of his "nine chapters on problems world-wide and Czech," which comprise his book *O smysl dneška* (On the Meaning of To-day), first published in 1969 and then pulped. It was only in March 1987 that this work was finally published by *Rozmluvy* (Conversations).

Patočka's reflections are straightforward, and precisely for that reason are frequently neglected. A writer's job is, first and foremost, *literature*, the communication of a literary expression by means of language. This is obviously not the everyday spoken tongue, nor the one that provides information in documents and newspapers. Nor is it the language of concepts and precise definitions used in the sciences and philosophy. According to Patočka, literature has a third path, to search out "the meaning of existence and its formal expression in the natural language." He sums up: "The creative writer is not . . . solely a man of imagination and 'ideas' created in literary form, or of stories incarnated in conceptualized ideas; the writer is a *revealer of life*, of the meaning of being, both general and particular."

And that is not all: according to Patočka, the writer is not only a "revealer of life," he is "a trustee, a manager . . . of the meaning of that life which is infrangible and personally accomplishable." That is why literature cannot be replaced by "any other activity of the spirit—sciences, philosophy or religion." And within the modern world, with its increasing "specialization and individual dispersion," the importance of literature is accordingly augmented by "the need to compensate, by memory of a homogeneity of life, and by a search for total rapport with the universe."

The responsibility which derives from such a concept of literature is quite different from that imposed upon writers by ideologues and politicians, who see only their own interests and goals. This is a role which issues from the intrinsic meaning of literature and which searches for the meaning of life, and which strives to reestablish or defend its integrity. One can, of course, include in this attempt every aspect of life, even politics and other practical matters—always with the proviso that a respect for this fundamental meaning, about which we have just spoken, continues to subsist within the literary work. In conclusion, the responsibility of the writer is the same as the responsibility of the free man who finds it repugnant to follow the orders of others and who prefers to listen to his own conscience; it is a responsibility which refuses to come to terms with any authorities whatsoever, and which searches within truth itself for a touchstone.

Czech literature can furnish us with many remarkable examples. Let me cite the work of Václav Havel, where variations on the theme of responsibility are preponderant. It could be said, without exaggeration, that this is the chief theme of many of his plays, and even the majority of his essays. One of these essays is, in fact, dedicated to the theme of responsibility. It is a reflection on the novel *Czech Dreambook*, and its author Ludvik Vaculík. In the essay Havel reveals his own conception, and that of Vaculík, of the writer's role in the modern world. For Havel, as well as for Vaculík and a number of other authors in this category, each personal work has as its point of departure an actual experience. This experience leads not only to what Patočka calls the revelation of "the meaning of being, both general and particular," but also to a defense of "the homogeneity of life, and a total rapport with the universe." He again brings up this point in his essay "The Writer's Thing."

In our search for the meaning of existence and our defense of the integrity of life, we are inevitably confronted by all those nonliterary aspects in Czechoslovakia which are summed up under the term *dissent*. We must, however, understand that this fact stems from the fundamental responsibility of the writer with regard to his work—a responsibility which is thus intertwined with his destiny. Václav Havel summed it up in a sentence applicable not only to Vaculík's *Czech Dreambook* but to Havel's own entire oeuvre: "The *Czech Dreambook* appears, from this viewpoint, to be a novel about responsibility, will and destiny—responsibility that is, if I may put it that way, stronger than will. It is a novel about the tragedy that arises from this responsibility; about the futility of all human efforts to break out of the role that responsibility has imposed; about responsibility as destiny."

Antonin Liehm   I am, as you know, a Czech, and the Czechs are not very good at exile. They haven't the tradition of, let's say, the Poles or the Hungarians. The Czechs are more like the French in this respect. They stayed home. Czech intellectual emigration is almost entirely a twentieth-century phenomenon.

A Pole will say, "Poland is where I am." But not a Czech. Czechoslovakia has no equivalent of *Polonia*, no tradition of two literatures. Poles have a great romantic literary tradition created outside the borders of Poland; Russians have a tradition of a literature written abroad; Czechs do not.

In the seventeenth century, before the birth of the Czech nation, the creation of national entities, national literatures and languages, we had a tradition of Protestant exiles. One of them was the great European intellectual, Comenius. The story of Comenius, a priest who left the country of his birth, still moves every Czech to tears. There is even a small monument in Moravia, a little piece of lawn; and this site, which is visited by pilgrims, is said to be where Comenius said farewell to his country, to take refuge (he a Protestant) first in Catholic Poland, and later in Holland. He became the first (and probably the only) great Czech writer and intellectual in exile. He became a European writer in exile. His origins were Czech, but his subsequent experience was that of exile and service to humanity, to European humanity, in a language which was to a large extent the lingua franca of Europe at that time—Latin.

This brings me to the great question: what is going away all about? What are we looking for? What do we want to be? Or to become, or to remain? Who are we, after we have been living and working abroad for ten, twenty, thirty years? For each of us the experience is different. There are no two similar experiences of exile, I believe. And there are no two similar experiences of different exiles.

Mr. Edwards mentioned an exiled Chilean writer sipping coffee in Santiago. To those of us who are exiles from Czechoslovakia, Poland, or the Soviet Union, that seems unreal. It is a different kind of exile. Yet both are real states of exile.

So are we going to remain what we were? Can we remain what we were? Are we becoming something different? Should we try to integrate ourselves into this new culture? How can we, if our instrument is a language in which we cannot communicate directly? Will we be accepted? Probably not. Can we switch languages? That's a different subject. Should we join the émigré ghetto of ethnic communities? That again is another thing. What can we do? What can we bring with us? Can we really bring something truly new to the dimension of humanity?

There is, of course, the value of what is called testimony. We can bear witness to our experience. That's fine. But we have all seen this testimony become transformed into exploitation. We are asked to testify, not because people are really interested in us and our experience, but because they want us to exorcise their own fears and obsessions. We have all been through that and we are all a little fed up with it. I speak for myself here, but I know others who feel the same way.

We attend conferences where we are supposed to recite the horrors of totalitarianism and of Soviet communism and everything else, because that is what we have done in the past. Now everybody knows, and those who don't know aren't interested. What we need is another dimension to our own existence.

Exile is an unknown. For each of us, exile has been a new experience, something previously unimaginable. Some have written about it. But can exile really be material for literature? And how far can it be material in literature? How far can this experience be communicated? Some have done it. Many have not. Take the German emigration during the Nazi period as an example. Thomas Mann built himself a house in California, a castle if you like, and continued his Germany in his literature as before. This was his dimension of emigration, and he refused to come back, because he took his country's literature with him. Only a few can follow his example.

All my life I have been a newspaperman, a journalist, and I love my work. Before I left, I wrote in several languages, and I thought that I could continue doing that. I very quickly found this was not the case, that to make a living I had to find a new job. I did not abandon my profession, but it took me fifteen years to be integrated into the new community.

The last point that I would like to make is that there is a mythology of exile—less, I believe, among exiles than among those who watch them. An exile means profit. An exile is somebody who may possibly be able to do something for humanity which others cannot. I don't have much faith in that. Few exiles think of themselves in that way (although some do, and we know who they are). The majority, however, have a rather modest idea of their existence and of their proper usefulness. Some manage to do one thing, but very few transform their particular experience, their particular landscape, into a *theatrum mundi*. They are not liked for that. Remember Joyce or Ibsen. Back home, they were considered unpatriotic.

So who then are we after twenty or thirty years spent abroad? When Roman Jakobson, the most cosmopolitan of the cosmopolitan émigrés in this century, was eighty years old, I spent a day with him at Harvard, and we talked and talked, and ate and drank, and late in the evening I asked him how he managed to speak and write so many languages. "You know," he replied, "when I dream, I dream in Russian; when I write about linguistics, I write in English; when I am sick, I ask that a French novel be brought to me; when I think about politics, I think in Czech" (because he spent his political years in Czechoslovakia); "I speak Polish with my wife. And then, there is German and Danish, and all that." "Roman," I asked, "who are you?" And he looked at me and said, *"Russky lingvist"* (a Russian linguist), and that, I believe, is God's honest truth.

I live in Paris; I have an American passport. And after twenty years I can speak several languages, but who am I? A Czech newspaper man. And that is not going to change.

William Gass   Are there any responses to those remarks? The implications are serious. Among them, of course, is the possibility that there is no general term "exile" that is appropriate, that it is an accidental and relatively trivial description, since, as I understand it, it is being suggested that every so-called exile's experience is fundamentally different, in which case the name would simply hide the differences. How much in common do we have?

Virgil Tanase   I agree with what Mr. Liehm has just said and would like to add a few words in context. My own experience may be instructive.

We have been talking about exile as a personal experience, but I wonder whether the term that has brought us together today may not have been invented by others. That is to say, there is no consensus among us that has made us into exiles. I am called an exile, but I never felt it as a problem. It's true I have left a country, Rumania, and a language; but in Rumanian culture there's a long tradition of writing in other languages, and I would not like to see the political experience I had to undergo obscure a fundamental question. If conditions had been otherwise, would I have left my country and language anyway? Rumanian is, after all, a language I love and in which I wrote with great delight, because it allows more scope than French for artful and sensual literary games. I left for a very simple reason—I belong to a small culture that from time to time feels the desire, the temptation, the arrogance to confront the great writers of humanity. To do so one must arrive at a common denominator: a major language.

A series of more or less accidental circumstances brought me to Paris, where I happened to ask for political asylum. In the interest of administrative convenience, I became a French citizen. Ultimately, I found myself defined as an exile. But I assure you that this never presented itself to me as a problem. In talking to other people, I have noticed that they assume that anyone who leaves a totalitarian country must be an exile.

The term is a kind of suitcase in which one can put anything. When I take off my shoes in the evening, I exile myself from my shoes. It is as simple as that. Fernando Arrabal left Spain because he had problems, and then Spain changed governments, and people stopped thinking of Arrabal as an exile. I think that, whether we like it or not, the word has acquired a connotation of prohibition—a political connotation that is foisted on it by other people and that may have no connection to us.

William Gass We might be able at this point to distinguish certain types of exiles, in terms of whether people were drawn out or pushed out, and whether, when they were pushed out, they pushed themselves out by creating problems which they then fled to avoid. Do we have any other commonalities?

Nuruddin Farah I have just been going through the biographies of the persons who are here, and have discovered one other common denominator. Almost ninety-nine percent of those present (excluding myself) have had long love affairs with their own governments. Many people here held positions of power as directors of schools, professors, etc. Then the relationship soured, and a period of internal exile began. It was only after this that they left the country.

I wonder if there is an analogy here with marriage, where a couple first falls out and then begins to say terrible things about each other.

Jan Vladislav   Isn't there also such a thing as interior exile?

Antonin Liehm   A word about what Mr. Farah mentioned—divorce. Kundera says that we all pursue the idea of vengeance, that every human being is obsessed with it. Children say: "I'll call my father," "I've got a big brother, and he'll (of course) show you." The man who divorces his wife and the wife who divorces her husband both seek revenge on the person whom he or she loved, and eventually stopped loving, and who has, of course, now become a horrifying creature.

You are right in a way. In every exile, as in every human being, there is, when he leaves, a thirst for vengeance: "I'll show you," or "I'll tell the others all about you." Eventually, of course, we have all discovered the futility of that particular fantasy. We have learned there is no vengeance; there is only our own truth, and our own life, and our own peace. We have discovered that, if other people are interested in our vengeance, it is not for our sake, but for theirs. So there is a parallel with divorce. I believe that the sour smell, the taste that remains on your tongue after you have taken your vengeance, is also the same in exile as in divorce.

William Gass   One puts one's spouse in a novel, and gets even in fiction, but isn't it true that, if we are sufficiently impotent in the political realm, we return to the page, to the imagination, where we can control events and cause things to happen as we wish? That's one great advantage, of course, of suffering injustice—it provides material. There are such people as injustice collectors.

I'd like to ask a question about so-called "interior exile": the image called up is one of leaving one place and going to another; and presumably you are not simply going off on a vacation. How do you do that—internally? What is the mechanism of leaving?

Virgil Tanase   When one is in exterior exile, there are borders which one may not cross. When one is in interior exile (and I have known that experience), one creates boundaries around oneself which others may not cross. It's as simple as that.

Jan Vladislav   I can only confirm what Mr. Tanase has just said. It was the same in Czechoslovakia.

It is often not exile that is the problem, but people who look on us as exiles. In France, for example, even if I spoke French very well (I don't), people would still say: "Ah, yes, you have a slight accent." That is to say, I am thought of as a foreigner, an exile—especially if people know my background. In countries like Czechoslovakia or Rumania, you are considered a dangerous person, a sort of criminal, and a boundary is put up around you, like that described by Tanase.

During the Soviet occupation of Czechoslovakia, I happened to be in France. Afterwards I returned to Czechoslovakia. One day, I remember saying: "We are like the Jews. Other people see us as Jews, as exiles, as foreigners who don't really belong completely in Czech society (or in any other)." Even in your own country, you can find you are an exile. You can be made into an exile, an alien, or a Jew by the opinion of other people.

Jiří Gruša   He was quoting me. I would like to attempt to sum up what I understand by the term "exile." It is said of the exiled writer that he is a person who has lost everything except his accent.

Jiří Gruša

The Portable Ghetto

―――――

People born in Bohemia at the end of the 1930s might see their lives as having passed under the sign of the portable ghetto. This could also be described as a review of a thrice-lost time.

We all know about lost time. The classic example (*le temps perdu*) might better be described as a past which did not take place in agreement with our plans. Our past could also be described as an ever-changing, ever-growing estrangement from our lives. We begin as nothing more than a plan, and by the end we have become a naked fact, a total reality divorced from its totality.

This is a truism which the writer, at least, has always attempted to defy. We might, more accurately, call him the ballad singer, the minstrel, the expert on that which was, and on its preservation. Since an important part of the Czech soul is Celtic, we might simply call the writer a bard.

As long as the bard dealt only with classic lost time, as long as he created a mutually accepted fiction of the past, he was not threatened with the ghetto as a permanent address. He was sought after. With his aid, forgotten deeds reappeared from the limbo into which they later again subsided, according to the dictates of fate. The bard stood before the crater of the underworld, fished out these deeds, and recreated them. He slowed down their decline into oblivion, offered the world a chance to reassess them, a chance to praise or criticize them, and finally a chance to strive for the desired ending.

The kings, in whose hands lay the deeds of the present, were pleased and they raised up the bards (usually sons of the lower orders), allowing them a place of honor next to the throne. "Everywhere the minstrel found somebody who wanted to hear his virtues praised, so as to prolong his timeless spirit. As all things pass, life also melts away, but he who is praised gains honor, and his dignity is retained under the heavens." Here I cite—very freely—an old English epic which fascinated me years ago because of the proud language of those verbal magicians of yesteryear. The minstrels, however, recognized their limits and knew that power over the here and now was basically a matter for kings.

The singers were entrusted with the control of the elements, the taming of wild animals, and the (usually) short-term banning of men and ghosts. Such arts were useful. When Arion was captured by pirates and permitted to voice a last wish before his execution (and even that was patronage), he was clever enough to ask for permission to "tune his lyre a little." He so entranced the robbers with his song that they were unable to prevent his escape. He swam away "on a dolphin's back," thus expanding the long line of animal vehicles by which singers used to travel.

Even in those idyllic times poets were, of course, slaughtered and exiled (among them Ovid, the author of my quotation), but a ghetto, a forcible isolation for them as a species, did not yet exist. Their skills, what today would be called know-how, held them together, but this outsider condition was then only guild membership. Thus the bards formed an association of skilled fairy-tale makers. They possessed the "science of fiction," but they did not forget that yesterday's deed, as a whole, could be allowed to run a quite different course, despite the art of suggestion which permitted past events to happen anew. In other words, every story is lacking at its very core, because the reteller is no true master of time. Only the true Master of the Endless, the Godhead, has endowed the bards with the ability to create fiction, and he did this for his own purposes. This modest way of going about things lasted—at least in my regions, and also here in Vienna—until one of the newfangled fictioneers decided on the swan as a mode of transportation. The semigod and knight Lohengrin (actually, our old friend the bard) descends to human regions, because he longs for a "woman." It would be easy to grab the queen for himself, all the more so since she finds herself in a precarious situation. The actual meeting is much more problematical. Spurred on by the envy of fellow mortals, she asks the forbidden question and thus disobeys the rule that would have saved her. An Orphic saga must contain a faux pas. Somebody must look back. In the Lohengrin version, it is crucial that Euridice is punished—justifiably, of course, because a woman who does not at once recognize her savior's divinity, but asks where he comes from, is guilty.

Lohengrin's claims are truly revolutionary. He lays claim not only to a heavenly but to an earthly throne. But he does this so tamely that we can only guess what actually happened. Fear not, he will soon appear, and quite nonchalantly. But there is still some part of his story left for the writer to invent. The expert on "Once upon a time" must grow into an expert on "so it shall be," and "science fiction" must develop from the "science of fiction." But even this transformation will not suffice. The "so it shall be" must be transformed into a "so it is," a "fictional science." Not many people after the age of puberty retain an enthusiasm for Jules Verne, but when fifteen-year-old captains step into bright tomorrows as argonauts, they are inevitably confident of a secure insight into the future. And it is from this point that they acquire the right and the means to reveal it.

The modern fairy tale, wondrous as ever, is thus told as theory. Just imagine for a minute that *Das Kapital*, whose science was purely bardic, had been written in the same traditional manner as the verse of the young Marx.

The bardic skill within the guild has become independent. The divine chance of a precise entry into the happening and its plan has been replaced by a certainty that the plan has been recognized. From the artisan guild which produced the meaningful, truth-revealing fairy tale, there developed a fighting group of specialists on the transformation of reality into saga.

It was to be foreseen. At the beginning of this century my countryman Rilke still bathed the death of old kings in nostalgia and cried out, more astonished than angry: "There was nothing before I saw it!" Even as he did so, a rather well-read Russian was already forging the theory of the reflection of objective truth—by objective mirroring experts—and had conceived the transformation of this truth into its higher, "concrete" form; that is, into a fairy tale about the existing being already existent.

Rather than down into hell, Orpheus went to heaven. But since then the world has been filled with denizens from the underworld. The old and limited unity of triple times, pressed into a work of art, is now moved to an intensive-care station and artificially kept alive. In the past we took for granted three, basically separate spheres of existence: the past with the underworld and the bard, the present with the earth and the king, the future with the heavens and the prophet. Under the trinitarian rule of Orpheus, who represents poetry, kinghood, and prophesy, the world has fallen into the hurricane of unleashed timelessness. The future is passed off as the present, thus transforming the present into an ineluctable past which one would like to forget. Eventually, one does forget it. And the past? It is simply cancelled.

But there, where plan and deed have already been agreed on from the start, life unfolds before the individual only on an optical level. Seen in reality, life is a mere subdivision of the hours to be wasted, a maze of lost opportunities, Potëmkin's super-village of stage fronts. That is what I understand by the concept of "time lost once again." That is where the ghetto for saga-singers begins, in as far as they were unable to cooperate in the assembly of a myth of the future. The reason is obvious: when you sing an old song, the new world shakes on its foundations. It rests solely on language, on the renaming of everything that exists. When you call a spade a spade, you are turned into a foreigner and stigmatized as a Jew.

Please permit me a personal recollection. My interrogator had already posed every question, including the one put to Lohengrin, about the origin of the singer, the author.

" 'Scuse me, are you Jewish?"

It was a surprise. If the man had found any such evidence, he'd not be querying a second time. He was obviously uneasy.

"Why do you think I am?" the author countered.

"Well, because everything seems to annoy you."

The author grew pensive. Why is it, he wondered, that this should be thought of as a Jewish trait?

"No, sir, I am a Slav . . . a Slav like you."

And I remembered a quotation from the chief Slavic language, a quotation which must have had its origin in a similar feeling. It was a sob of Marina Tsvetaeva: "All poets are Yids." So you take up your ghetto. But no matter how typical, this ghetto still fails to offer any real experience of time, which is lost for a third time. Many inside dream of countries where the Once, the Now, and the Afterward have flowed side by side since ancient times with only rare interminglings. The dream is similar to the myth of a miraculously preserved Golden Age.

Sometimes you can even break out of the ghetto world. You may even be chucked out on your ear. You catch your breath and lo, you find people who show interest in you and who see you (more or less correctly) as a future colleague. Since, for the most part, however, their main motivation is their own future importance, they would like you to confirm that the new struggle for heaven is more worthy, more honorable than the old struggle against hell. They expect you to confirm too that the uneasiness they feel in the world is by no means the original vocation of the caste of singers, but a systematic effort to victimize them personally. Woe to you if you do not agree with them.

But this is by no means the worst that will happen to you. Among the stream of awkward encounters lurking just around the corner, yet more dire is the one with the local futurologists. They declare the traumatic ghetto experience over there to have been a communication breakdown, to be assessed statistically. In a subjective sense, it may well have seemed momentous and even difficult, but objectively you have no grounds for complaint. Only *they* know the way. For a long while you are patient, but there comes a time when you tell them to go to hell. They freeze, retreat a step or two, and from their new perspective they see it . . . the Yellow Star.

You yourself have not noticed it, you simply forgot all about it, but now you see you've never gotten rid of it.

The ghetto has been transformed into a circus cart that you push ahead of you all over the world.

Soon you notice other vagrants camping in fields outside the towns and villages, and it occurs to you that you might assemble a merry company from them, even if not a particularly fashionable one. The idea doesn't go down at all well. Some of the vagrants have been exiled because they failed to create a sufficiently cozy fiction, others have brought their bitter quarrels with them, and still others allow themselves to be led around by the nose. Their various states of exile are all quite different. At last you decide to throw in your lot with those men and women who have experienced something similar . . . to what you and I have experienced. These people are your siblings. There is a greater link between you and them than a joint camping ground or a few circus tricks. You even wonder whether these people—whether we ourselves—are not the new Salt of the Earth, part of a paradoxical plan of God to destroy the plans of the World Destroyers, the germ of a future community where the *fact* can once again be what it used to. But in the meantime you have had enough practice to be able to feel the invisible emblem on your coat almost automatically. Anyone can make out, without difficulty, the ancient prophetic freight behind this thought and thus a new version of the wandering Jew.

To anyone who asks me about anything other than the way through triply lost time, I have no answer. The only fact that sticks in my mind is the name of an extinct bird: *Didus ineptus*, or the Ancient Dodo.

Guillermo Cabrera Infante

The Invisible Exile

———

*I was born in Cuba, and I
hope to die in England.*

I live now in exiledom by the sea. Here I work and play, and even
watch other people work and play from the cozy vantage point of my
bay windows, which look out onto the bay. Here I read a romance
that is the story of my life. (A historian is only a writer with hind-
sight.) Ensconced in a comfortable chair by the fire, while, outside,
squalls made the street squalid, I began to read. "How horrible," said
a voice. "But what deviltry must happen to make a man invisible?"
"It's not deviltry," another voice responded. "It's a process." That's
what it is: a process, and it began some years ago. Now I too am
invisible. Not invincible, but the opposite. To be invisible means to
be as vulnerable as the unseen. You are less a person than a nonper-
son. You are pure spirit and you can be blown out like a candle in the
wind—and who's going to remember what kind of flame you were
before the candle was blown out? It is a metaphysical problem. Being
invisible, however, is a very physical thing to me. It happens, as it did
to that man Griffin, however, every time I take off my jacket (tweed),
my pullover (100 percent wool), my twill trousers, my usual suede
shoes. . . . (I must wear warmer clothes in my exiledom by the sea
than in the tropics, where I was born, where I chose exile rather than
become a pawn in a monstrous game of chess in which only one man
can play king.) Now I take off my underwear and I look at myself in

the full-length mirror. I look at myself in the mirror not once but twice—and I see a void. Nothing! Not a thing! Am I like the stranger who came into a pub on a winter night in England? Am I really *invisible*? I am fully dressed but everybody thinks I must be wearing a disguise, though I'm perfectly naked when I undress. If I get rid of my English garments nobody sees anything or everybody sees nothing, whichever comes off first. I am the reverse of that king who plays a murderous game of chess with his subjects. I am (and even the proverbial five-year-old can tell this) a Cuban exile. In my case, however, exile is more like *exit*. My clothes make an Englishman of me, but my nakedness erases me. I cannot find refuge in a nudist camp: the invisible nudist is an obscene Peeping Tom. I cannot even be a sight for sore eyes. I am myself if I wear my clothes. Just the invisible man in book and movie. Sometimes I think that I too am an invention of H. G. Wells. But even Wells went to Russia and couldn't see the invisible Russians, those who saluted Stalin because they were about to become invisible forever. Their chess king, bishops and commissars and all the knights and red pawns were the only Russians visible to Wells. It's a dirty trick, but it has happened so many times in this century of voiceless invisible men that nobody cares any longer.

The Romans, not the Greeks, had a word for the invisible man; they invented him. His name was Ovid and when the Romans had seen him once or twice they never saw him again. He was too busy making himself the perfectly invisible poet. He was, in any case, the perfect exile. Or rather the perfectly visible Roman courtier who became invisible in exile. The Russian Empire has a few of those. The most visible invisible man in Russia was, of course, Osip Mandelstam. Stalin made him invisible with the deadly accuracy of a magic wand.

As for me (a nonpoet), invisible is not the word to define my status. Even the Latin word is different when it applies to a Cuban. Before, in Cuba (BC, which means Before Castro), the Republican refugees from the Spanish Civil War (even Pablo Casals and Juan Ramón Jiménez were there, briefly) were called *exilados*. Now all the Spanish-speaking exiles are called *exiliados*. Perhaps you don't mind that little change, but I do. All Cubans do. We must remind the world of those stubborn Jews who in another diaspora fled from Hitler. The

Jews were not exiles. They were not even Jewish, because that word suggests they were slightly Jews. Remember the ordeal of Walter Benjamin before the gates of Spain? He was not a German and not quite a Jew.

We are not *marranos* (pigs), we are *gusanos* (worms), and those Cubans expelled from Cuba via Mariel, 120,000 of them in one short month in 1980, were called *escoria* (scum). Goebbels used to call all Jews *Ungeziefer* (vermin), which is not by chance what Gregor Samsa is called in *The Metamorphosis*. It is easier to eliminate a man when he is not a man but scum from the slums, a worm, *Ungeziefer*. But there are always bloodstains, I'm afraid, a mess to clean up. It is cleaner, therefore, and more desirable, to make an invisible man out of him—and "out of him" is the operative phrase. My invisibility is more visible in Spain, in the Spanish-speaking countries, and among Hispanics in the U.S.A. There is in Spain a great authority on rendering almost anything invisible. It is the Big Brother (or rather Big Mother) of the language, and it's called the "Royal Academy of the Spanish Language." The *Academia*, as she is called, for she is an old and respectable lady, is a shredding machine that is kept very busy eliminating the undesirable. The dictionary of the *Real Academia* is Big Mama's troubleshooter. Troubleshooters, as we all know, can become accurate hit men. Each word in the language is a contract to be shot off if the *Academia* doesn't love it or even like it. The *Academia* particularly dislikes foreign words or words to that effect, such as most Americanisms. Those words are sitting ducks, and a word that is not in the dictionary is a dead duck. Or it should be pronounced dead, as in a dead tongue. All words are suspect, or guilty, until proven innocent. Let's now consider now the word "exile." Exile is not a Spanish word. Never heard of it, said the *Academia*; I don't know what it means.

There are, of course, words for exile in Spanish: *exilio*, which is the condition of exile, as in the case of the Roman poet or what Ovid saw. An *exiliado* is an exile or what Stalin did to Mandelstam for a poem he wrote. An offshoot of the dictionary is the *Manual*, which is very much like the *Concise Oxford Dictionary*, but made palatable with illustrations and diagrams. This dictionary has something of the spirit of the comic strips—not, I must say, a Spanish invention, though it has a Spanish antecedent. Alphabet charts in Cuban schools always began with a big cross, and when reading the primer aloud, the young student had to say "Christ, ABC," etc. Christ came before letters, that is, before words. That too was an invention of the *Academia*. Little did the Old Prude know that Christ could be a swear word!

On page 711, column A, the dictionary performs a *grand jeté* and jumps from *exiguo* to *eximio*. In between these graciously bandied legs the dictionary inserts a suppository called *eximente*. That is from "eximent," to excuse oneself. Hey, presto! Exile has disappeared and all exiles are sent to (S)Iberia: a *Léger de main* or *léger des humains*?

My edition of the *Diccionario* is by Espasa Calpe, printed in 1950 when Franco was king. To Franco there was no exile. Exiles simply didn't exist. There were only enemies rapidly running for cover. As that other grotesque dwarf King Ubu used to say, "If there is no Poland, there won't be any Poles." [The reference is to Alfred Jarry's play *Ubu Roi.*—ed.] Jaruzelski might be advised to meditate on this axiom. If there are no Poles there won't be a Polish problem. "Solidarity" would dissolve into a dew. Heard on the BBC: "Today Poland went to the polls."

For those who believe that tomorrow is a better world (it is not even a better *word*), in 1956 the big *Diccionario de la Real Academia* finally admitted exile—but not exiles. This dictionary, which moves ahead in reverse gear, is still revered by many writers in the Spanish-speaking world. One of those admirers was a very well known literary critic from Uruguay, who died in a plane accident. Before he died he wrote the longest article ever on political exiles in Latin America, and he named only one exile from Cuba. That exile was José Martí, and he died in Cuba in 1895! Later a laureate writer from Colombia made a speech before another academy, not on literature but on exiles. He chose Chile as the Latin American country that bans the most people from its territory. He quoted figures: one million Chileans emigrated, leaving Pinochet to rule alone over the condor, the Chilean vulture. He cried out loud, "It's decimation!" and finished his speech with not a single mention of Cuba. There are no exiles from Cuba. As we know, this is a model country when it comes to dissidents and malcontents, who are usually going, rather than coming. Fidel Castro is an exquisite tyrant. If you don't believe it, see how he treats his opponents. He has a motto, "Semper Fidelis," which most Cubans read as "Sic semper Fidelis."

But truth is always buoyant and it surfaces in the murkiest waters. Since 1959 about a million and a half Cubans have gone into exile, including, as a tropical Kerensky, the island's first revolutionary president. Only now does Cuba have more than ten million inhabitants. So it is more than decimation. It is a decimation and a half. But all this is unmentionable. You cannot call Cuba a tyranny, because it is a Third World tyranny. In the Third World tyrannies are always called developing countries, and the crimes the tyrant commits are mere *accidents de parcours*, as the French so elegantly put it. An Argentine writer living in Paris all his adult life was asked by a French newspaperman about Cuban writers in exile and he answered with a French accent: "There are no exiled writers from Cuba. There are only worms abroad." A worm in Spanish is also a caterpillar, and the risk involved in exiling caterpillars is that they can become butterflies. This Argentine writer, now deceased, was very close to Marx, but very far from Linnaeus.

A group of political refugees gathering in Madrid recently had what you can call a worm's eye view. They were from every Spanish-speaking country: from all of them, that is, except Cuba. Nobody at the party missed the Cubans, who had been in exile longer than all the rest put together. Curiouser and curiouser! said a local Alice. The meeting was an occasion for party goers to have a political fling. They even called exile an acquired taste—like caviar. Here, have some: caviar from the General (who could be Pinochet or Stroessner). Some canapés? It's for the sake of the party, the political party. Some *vol-au-vents*? They keep the exile spirit flying.

Hmmm! It's delicious! It's delightful! It's delovely! It all seemed like inverted nostalgia for Franco. Ah, those were the days, my friend! See here, have some oysters and you won't feel ostracized. This elixir of exile was Spanish, but it also exists in the collective mind. Cuba cannot be as dreadful as all that. You left your island paradise simply because you want to live abroad: you must miss the wine and all those tall blonde girls. Get back, get back to where you once belonged. Cubans, go home.

The Cuban minister for culture should have been called, like Goebbels, minister for enlightenment and propaganda. I know he exists because I've seen him in a photo wearing a dark pinstripe three-piece suit and he looked, I swear, like someone out of *The Godfather: Part Two*. He had a waspish lisp and his name could have been Mr. Malaprop. He once said on Cuban television that Fidel Castro was not ill, but simply tired out from a "pneumatic" in his lungs. He meant, of course, pneumonia! On another occasion when I introduced him to a particularly beautiful girl, he exclaimed: "She has perfect facial ovulation." He also says "hiralious" instead of "hilarious." He believes that it was Beethoven and not Van Gogh who lost an ear, and—very fittingly—when he wants to be intimate, he just intimidates. This is Cuba's minister of culture. As you can see, Fidel Castro is a tyrant with a sense of humor. This minister's name is Armando Hart and this Hart belongs to Daddy.

Dr. Hart—the tyrant and his minions really love it when he is called doctor—declared in the newspaper *El Pais* that no writer of "high stature" (his very words) had left Cuba after the Revolution. He named a few names: Fernando Ortiz, Alejo Carpentier and Lezama Lima, and managed to pronounce them all without a wisp of a lisp. But he forgot to say that all the aforementioned writers remained in Cuba simply because they now live underground. You see, they all died many years ago. I can add to those egregious names that of Virgilio Piñera, Cuba's greatest playwright, who stayed behind to die, like most internal exiles, of fear and neglect.

None of those writers can move unless they are carried on the shoulders of "politic worms," as Hamlet calls us. Otherwise, I don't see how they can leave the island. Unless of course they swim across the seas to become, in turn, invisible corpses in exile.

Then Dr. Hart, the minister of propaganda, exalted the memory of Lezama Lima, perhaps the greatest poet to write in Spanish this century. Dr. Hart mentioned *Paradiso*, a novel he couldn't read without moving his lips (lisp), but he never said that only 5,000 copies of this novel were printed in Lezama's lifetime. This is a fact, and I know why. Lezama praises homosexuality in his book, and that wouldn't do in a country where they built concentration camps for homosexuals. This double-backed bête noire was condemned publicly by Fidel Castro himself in 1971, in a famous/infamous speech. After that the bulky Lezama became an invisible internal exile.

Not even a letter by him was published after this Faustian condemnation by Mefisto-*fidel*. But Lezama wrote letters in invisible ink. He was still writing when he died. Most of those letters were written to his sister in exile in Puerto Rico, and she made them into a book. This epistolary legacy from the nether world shows a Lezama preoccupied not only with food and medicine, but also with the quality of life under socialism: "It is not the same," he wrote, "to be out of Cuba as to observe the life one is obliged to lead here inside the oven. There are Cubans who suffer outside and those who suffer equally here, even more so, being in the burning hole with the fearful anxiety of an uncertain fate."

Here we have words like "burning," "oven," etc. Don't they proclaim that the hermetic poet is speaking, not of paradise, but of hell, where the burning poet is some sort of condemned Faust? It was Lezama who defined the poet as a "possessed person penetrated by a soft hatchet." But what about the possessed poet who is denied all except the "killing axe?" Essence, existence, and even the solid body that contains his conscience are owned by the state. Lezama and Piñera are here with me, invisible men all. We are like the man who arrived at the *Coach and Horses* in a remote spot in England almost a century ago. This is how arrival and welcome are described by a man who knew about such things:

> "You don't understand . . . who I am or what I am. I'll show you." . . . He put his open palm over his face and withdrew it. The center of his face became a black cavity. . . . The nose—it was the stranger's nose—rolled on the floor with a sound of hollow cardboard. Then he removed his spectacles and everyone gasped. He took off his hat and with a violent gesture tore at his bandages. . . . A flash of horrible anticipation passed through the hall. . . . The stranger was an invisible man.

[The quotation is from *The Invisible Man*, by H. G. Wells.—ed.]

William Gass   I am reminded almost immediately of the novel by Ralph Ellison, *The Invisible Man*, which recounts many similar attitudes.

Horst Bienek

Exile Is Rebellion

──────────

I am probably the only one among us who is not an exile, even though I do feel a certain sense of belonging to your group. I am not an exile, although I have been forced to leave my country, my friends, and my way of life on two occasions. The first time was in May 1945, in Silesia—the land of my childhood; I was fifteen years old. The second time, while a pupil of Bertolt Brecht in the "berliner ensemble," I was arrested by the KGB and deported to Vorkuta, in Siberia. After nearly four years of forced labor, I was released to begin a new life in West Germany. By then I was twenty-five. I changed territories, countries, and governments—but not languages.

The loss of language is probably the most decisive factor in determining exile; it is what makes exile so wretched for the writer. In the process you lose almost everything: childhood, upbringing, mentality, myth. Even if the exile quickly learns the words of the new language, he still needs a long time to express himself on a literary plane in the new tongue. Nabokov began to write in English twenty years after he became an exile. After fifteen years of exile, Brodsky writes his prose in English, but his verse in Russian. Thomas Mann, who incidentally supposedly spoke English with a ghastly accent, composed his every sentence in German—after fifteen years of exile in the United States.

I was able to take my language with me. Aside from the forced-labor camp in Vorkuta, which was an exceptional situation, I found the German language and German readers at my place of arrival. Over the course of the last two or three decades a large number of East German writers have moved west, and we have frequently discussed the question of whether we are in exile or not. There are those who hold to this view—those, in particular, who regard themselves as Marxists or socialists. They were exiled from their milieu, from their ideology, from their circle of friends. I have never been able to accept their self-perception as exiles. Anyone who leaves the Catholic Church may experience loneliness and even feel lost, but he is not in exile. No, those of us who have left "The German Democratic Republic" for the "Federal Republic of Germany," that is, traded East Germany for West Germany, are not in exile. The word "exile" is too weighty, too momentous, too significant to be watered down in this fashion.

I am here because I have adopted the cause of exile, albeit from a different direction: as an entreaty, as a memory, as a call of conscience. This process of adoption has to do with German history. We must not forget that it was we Germans who forced into exile thousands, tens of thousands, even hundreds of thousands of people—writers, artists, scientists, the common people. We did this for religious, political, and racist reasons.

I remember reading, among my first books, about the difficult life of our exiles during the Nazi period. I read how André Gide failed to show up at the antifascist Writer's Congress in Paris in May 1935, because he had a dinner appointment with Ernst Jünger. Later I myself lived in the West—as an editor, a writer, and a member of various academies and clubs. And I saw, next to me, next to us, writers from different countries and languages who had fled to our country, only to suffer deprivation and need. Certainly I have in mind linguistic deprivation, but there is material deprivation as well. I refuse to allow myself to lapse into the role of an André Gide. When I think of Munich, all I see are André Gides. When I arranged a reading for exile authors (and their translators) in the Bavarian Academy of the Fine Arts, the hall was full, but I saw none of my German colleagues, who should have felt gratitude not to find themselves in exile. They are all a despicable pack of André Gides. But I cannot despise them, for if I were to do so, I would lose all my friends. Indifference had petrified the hearts of men whom I otherwise liked.

You may have noticed: I am always speaking of exiles. I recall Brecht's verse:

False—this name that others gave us:
"Emigrants" leave freely,
Selecting a new country.
We left not freely,
Searched for no country
To stay—perhaps forever.
We fled, were cast out, banished.
The land that receives us is no home,
It is exile.

In the Federal Republic of Germany we establish foundations, conduct conventions and symposia, edit journals and books, and generally spend millions to study the exiles of the 1930s. I have yet to hear of a congress in our country such as this one. Who gives a thought to the fact that the misery which then drove so many into despair, depression, and death touches upon the new exiles in equal measure? There are not fewer writers and artists than in the thirties, but more, and their need is no less. They write Russian, they write Czech, they write Hungarian, Rumanian, Polish, Bulgarian, Spanish. They live among us.

In the meantime the old period of exile has yet to come to an end. Hans Sahl, who emigrated to the United States and from there sent us wonderful translations of Thornton Wilder, Tennessee Williams, and Arthur Miller, wrote a poem:

We're the ones to ask
For the life descriptions of our friends.
They're written down on tiny cards
and crammed into little boxes
Dangling from our necks—belly high.
Research institutes vie for the laundry lists
Of those who are now lost.
Museums preserve the "subject headings" of our agony,
Like relics under glass.

So let us ask the question: how many of us were there then who could not pay their laundry bills . . . or the rent . . . or the gas? How many killed themselves?

Things are no different today. Such things happen in our city, perhaps on our street. Today's exiles live among us and, like then, cannot pay their laundry bills, the rent, the gas. I know some who have left the Federal Republic for France, Norway, the United States. I personally know two who committed suicide. They couldn't wait for the Volkswagen Foundation or the Thyssen Foundation or the German Research Society to discover, publicize and comment upon their (largely unpublished) testimony. All these institutions would do better to devote themselves to living, rather than dead, poets.

No, we must not search for exile in literary history. We have all failed. Allow me to name a few disparate examples. The Pole Jerzy Košinski, world-renowned author of *The Painted Bird*, spent the first ten years of his exile in Munich—unrecognized and even unknown. Then he left for New York, where he became internationally famous. Yefim Etkind, one of the most brilliant Russian literary scholars, waited in vain in Munich for a university appointment. He finally received a position in Nanterre and moved to Paris. The Polish philosopher Leszek Kołakowski hoped to become Jürgen Habermas's successor, but he followed a call to Oxford, even though he then spoke better German than English. Over the course of the last nineteen years the Czech poet Ivan Divis has lived in Munich and published some nineteen collections of verse. He is considered to be the greatest living Czech poet by his countrymen at home and in exile, but no German publishing house has gotten around to putting out a collection of his verse.

For every world-famous Milan Kundera there are a hundred other writers living among us who are not even published. A few are translated, only to go unnoticed by the critics and unread by the public. And there are no literary prizes for them. After all, they write in a different language.

All this being said, I am not prepared to sing a dirge to exile. Exile can also mean opportunity. Hilde Spiel, herself a former émigré, once remarked that "an exile must not necessarily live within an alien reality. His existence can take place on a higher plane, in a realm which is spiritual in nature, international . . . and, should he make the leap into the new idiom . . . surprising gains are to be made." Half of the Spanish-Iberian literature in this century has been written in exile. At any one point in time there have inevitably been dictatorships from which authors have fled—but they did not lose their environment or language in the process. The same is true of East German authors who have emigrated to West Germany. And I am not at all certain that Witold Gombrowicz, who has remained more Polish in his diaries than any Warsaw Pole, would have achieved the same international acclaim if he had remained in the cafés of Warsaw. The cosmopolitan nature of many great artists can be understood only within the context of exile—from Kandinsky to Schönberg from Silone to Koestler, beginning with the entire German school of Expressionism up to Wols and Rolf Nesch, to Neizvestny and Brodsky.

But a Russian exile writer will never escape his language. German and Russian are languages that one cannot abandon without paying a price in literary substance. And certainly the same is equally true of other, "small" languages which I know less well. The exile has a sense of having been cast out, pushed away, isolated . . . and he is right. He continues to write in his native language, but the people around him speak a different language. The poet can learn this language, but it is unlikely that it will serve him as an instrument of his creativity. Herein lies the paradox: the world of exile becomes the alibi of his existence. To find a homeland in his new language would uproot him.

No, this appeal is relevant to all of us: exile is not a condition. Exile should be a revolt. Exile must scream to be heard—scream in the face of our indifference. One day those of us who have settled down will be measured, not only by how we treated nature, but by how we treated man in exile as well. Exile is relevant to all of us.

Virgil Tanase In the spirit of contradiction, and also because I now come from France, a country which encourages contradictions, I cannot allow some of the things which have been said here to pass without comment. I must point out, first of all, that Mr. Bienek, who has not left his language behind, has allowed himself to speak on behalf of those who have. I find myself in a delicate situation here, because I have the impression that I am richer than he [in language]. Nevertheless, even though an imbalance of strength makes me reluctant to strike a blow, I will do just that.

To think of the literary language as a simple means of communication, a sort of language of the bistro, is not an astute way of looking on the writer's medium.

Although Rumanian is my mother tongue, the moment came when I realized that this language would be inadequate for communicating what I had to say. So I began to work and to play with this language, to do violence to it, to force words to work together, to make them destroy each other, so that they would say what I wanted them to say. At that time I was translating writers as diverse as Balzac and Gogol, and I had the same experience—that everyday Rumanian, the language we would use in a colloquium like this, did not say what literature wants to say.

I felt obliged, therefore, to learn the writer's language as if it were a foreign tongue. "There is no such thing as the Rumanian you write," people told me later. After that I did not simply change from Rumanian to French; I actually served an apprenticeship in another language.

The French I write is, I think, the literary French which a Frenchman must learn to write—with the same efforts, the same pains, the same difficulties as I myself had. I do not believe in the impoverishment which supposedly occurs when one moves from one language to another. I regard it even as an enrichment.

There are a number of examples of a poet writing in a language other than his own. There is Tzara, whose poems in Rumanian are unquestionably inferior to those which he wrote in French. In Germany there is Paul Celan, and in France we have Cioran and Ionesco.

The second point I would like to mention is the difficult condition of the exiled writer. When I began to write in French, I came up against the problems all French writers encounter, and they were even greater than those which I experienced when writing as an exile.

My work is admittedly rather recondite, and I often wonder if I would not encounter even greater difficulties if I were a native Frenchman. There is, in other words, a certain prejudice on the part of the press which acts in my favor, and this, I believe, is not always a bad thing. I do not believe we should make out exile to be a state of inevitable misery. The difficult writer who does not sell more than a thousand copies might well encounter the very same publishing difficulties if he were French or Spanish or Hungarian.

Libuše Moníková   I come from Prague, but I have lived in West Germany since 1971 and I write in German. I would like to make the following comments on this change of country and language: It was, in fact, the experience of exile that inspired me to write—the experience of things that had previously been alien and remote from me.

A number of points come to mind. In Czechoslovakia I studied German language and literature; I even received my doctorate in that field, but that does not mean that I had mastered the language. When I first arrived in West Germany, I began to write in Czech, but I realized that I was caught in a double trap—that of topic and that of language. My themes were difficult to approach; I felt as if I were raping them. And I realized how locked in I was by the language; I sensed an inability to find the right words, a lack of sufficient distance. So I stopped . . . and began again in German. My German was hardly of a high literary level and could not take me very far, but nevertheless it helped me to acquire that greater distance which I craved. I kept testing what I had written to see if it was accurate, and I found I was better able to describe certain physical circumstances and sensations in German than in Czech. Thus, in my case at any rate, strangeness led me to greater precision. I even had the advantage of not having grown up with German clichés—in written German, that is—and I thus was able to employ these clichés consciously for stylistic purposes.

There was yet another factor which prevented me from writing in Czech. I had an enormous respect for that strange language, which makes even major writers, like Kafka, sound sober and down to earth. When I first read Kafka, it was in Czech, and I was very disappointed. Kafka was very Czech—very sparse and unspectacular, very sober and lean. It was only when I read Kafka in German that I realized his importance, and that it is these very sober Czech elements in his work which are so spectacular.

So I can say that it was Kafka who gave me the courage to write in German, since our situations were, to some extent, comparable. His active vocabulary is not all that large, but he was virtually the only one of the Prague German writers who was able to cope with his literary household, using these sparse means. During that same period Werfel and Max Brott were attempting to enrich their use of language by leafing through Baroque anthologies and using expressions that had become virtually obsolete. Kafka was the only one consistently to use this lean language. The language which had developed by that time was the Czech he heard all around him, the living language.

I do not claim that loss of language is an outright advantage, but it is fundamentally bound up with a sense of loss and sorrow. More than anything, it is work. But in certain situations there are advantages to be derived.

For my part, I can say that the change of languages has been of benefit to my writing.

Jan Vladislav   One of our greatest forerunners, Dante, spoke Italian as his native language, but the language which he used to write in was Latin. In a poem written in Italian, he says expressly that this was an experiment, that it was not the custom. This admission was significant. His friend, or rather his successor Petrarch (also an émigré), wrote all his personal letters in Latin—as well as his observations and personal, even erotic, notes. But he wrote his poems in Italian.

Edward Limonov

*Thirteen Studies
on Exile*

———

[1] In Russian the word
"exile" has such a pompous ring to it that I haven't got the *chutzpa* to
apply it to my own modest six-year existence in New York, and my
seven further years in Paris. That stolid, bourgeois, fat-assed word
"exile" might have been applicable to the nineteenth-century noble-
man Alexander Herzen, and certainly fits Solzhenitsyn, the family
man, who even managed to bring his furniture out with him. As for
me, I've always felt like a poor student or a member of the working
class, someone who lives in rented rooms—like a character in a novel
by Dostoevski.

I was first "exiled" in 1967, from Kharkov to Moscow, just as I
later "exiled" myself from New York to Paris. Anyone who gives any
thought to the word "exile" will come to the conclusion that contemporary Russian émigré writers (and I include myself here) have no
right to call themselves exiles. We are what might be called self-
exiles.

Neither do I consider myself a "political refugee" from the Soviet
regime. My fellow émigrés have the political pull of their rich American uncles to thank for that status. When push came to shove, I fled
from that Paradise too, with its smell of Kentucky Fried Chicken and
greasy cholesterol. I emigrated.

Being a modest type, I consider myself just a writer living in
Paris. Like Joyce. Like Hemingway. Like Scott Fitzgerald, Saroyan,
Baldwin . . . and many others.

[2]   Life abroad is a lot more interesting than in the country where you were born and grew up, if only because the newness is so stimulating. If I had my druthers, I would like to live many lives, each in a different country. Despite the petty inconveniences involved, I am fascinated by the process of getting to know a new country, its ways, language, mores, the primitive or sophisticated brainwashing methods used by those in power to keep the rebellious masses under control. And having lived now in three countries—the USSR, the U.S.A., and France—I really am unable to answer the question: "Which is best?" All of them have become part and parcel of my own personal history. From a professional point of view, France is more to my liking than the U.S.A. or the USSR, inasmuch as France has a traditional respect for the text, the written communication, the book. I perceive the text of a novel to be just that—a text, with no ideological riders clinging to it (contrary to the view of the ruling philologists in the U.S.A. and the USSR). But we shall see what we shall see. I am now writing a book, the action of which takes place in France. Let's see if the local authorities will be as offended by this foreigner as were the American authorities.

[3]   If I'm not mistaken, I am the only Russian writer who has carved out a writer's career for himself without the aid of anti-Sovietism after leaving the USSR. It's not for me to judge the quality of what I write, but I take pride in having done it myself, without the assistance of any political party or any other groups.

Even the cult of Brodsky-the-decadent-poet rests on the foundation laid by the trial of Brodsky-the-parasite. The profession of "poet" was not recognized by the judge as a legitimate occupation in his case. He became a celebrity thanks to the (not so much cruel as stupid) conduct of the authorities, who forgot that the West scrutinizes what goes on in the USSR under a magnifying glass. Solzhenitsyn-the-mediocre-writer ought to divide his royalties with the Soviet authorities in gratitude for the colossal publicity campaign they provided for him by sending him into exile. Even if he were to do so, however, it would never be enough to reward adequately the Western press and Western circles hostile to the USSR for the publicity they showered on his tardy, unjust, and hysterical criticism of Soviet society.

Russian literature has, in a sense, been force-fed with politics. The Russian writer is automatically expected to be either exclusively Soviet or exclusively dissident. If a Russian "exile" writer turns out to be more complex than the Soviet/anti-Soviet model, his life and the fate of his books become more complicated in like proportion. I had to survive seven years and *thirty-five* rejections from American publishing houses to see my novel *It's Me—Eddie* in print in the United States. And even as the rejections rolled in, all sorts of "exposés" of the Soviet Union made their way to an American publisher without any difficulty. Soviet publishing houses manifest the same delight in regurgitating a novel about the life-style of the American unemployed.

[4] It is, in some ways, uncomfortable to find yourself forced into the role of a Russian writer in exile. The entire world, in my view, pays far too much attention to the activities and internal policies of the USSR. Every random philistine who's read his share of cheap newspapers imagines himself to be a Kremlinologist and irritates the Russian writer in exile with vituperations over the KGB, the Gulag, Siberia, Afghanistan, Poland, and God only knows what other sort of rot. I can't stand that sort of attention; I feel as if I were a Roman, and as such responsible for everything that Rome did, or did not do. Not infrequently, you are liked or disliked simply because you are a Roman (Russian), and therefore a son of that powerful state, albeit it a prodigal one.

Once, in a discotheque in Nice, someone learned that I was Russian and called me a pig. Graciously, I forgave this untypical representative of the French people his barbarity. Sometimes I use English as camouflage and pass myself off as an American. Still, that's a tricky game because, if roughly one-half of the world's population doesn't like Russians, the other half is hostile to the Yankees. Nowadays I try to pass myself off as an Albanian writer in exile.

[5] Having been through the struggle for existence in three countries (and not in the form of package tours or diplomatic junketing), I do not share the multiplicity of prejudices, phobias, and myths extant in the world. I do not, for example, perceive a great difference in the life of ordinary people in most countries. Under any political

system the working man (I was a working stiff for twenty years) puts in his eight hours a day. The social system has yet to be invented which will free him from these eight unpleasant hours of daily slavery. Both in the USSR and in the U.S.A. millions of people wolf down their breakfasts and rush off to work. Perhaps the Soviet worker is more poorly dressed and his breakfast less nutritious than that of his alter ego in the U.S.A., and perhaps he travels to work in a bus rather than in his own car, but such differences are hardly sufficient cause for two peoples to fling atom bombs at each other.

And what about the Soviet threat to the West? I don't believe it exists. The U.S.A. and Europe, together, are twice as strong as the USSR. The two world wars were launched by Western democracies, and not by the USSR. No Soviet soldier has ever occupied one inch of U.S. territory, whereas in 1919 the United States sent an "expeditionary force" into Soviet territory. The USSR has never used nuclear weapons, whereas in 1945 the United States introduced a sinister era by dropping atomic weapons on the civilian populations of Hiroshima and Nagasaki. If we dig deeper into history, we will uncover other invasions of Russia by the West: 1812, 1855, 1918, 1919, 1920, 1921, 1941 . . . Any objective observer would have to conclude that it is Russia who should fear the West, and not the contrary.

I believe it would be useful to send future heads of state (incognito, of course) into exile for a few years into the supposedly hostile country. This would liberate them from provincialism, phobias, and prejudices.

[6]   I did not find the freedom to be a radical opponent of the existing social structure in the country which pompously calls itself the "leader of the free world," but neither did I notice it in the land which represents itself as "the bright future of all humanity." The FBI is just as zealous in putting down American radicals as the KGB is with its own radicals and dissidents. True, the methods of the FBI are more modern. They don't arrest dissidents, for this would transform them into celebrities by the next morning. All glory to the FBI! The KGB, however, is studying the techniques of its older brother and is successfully modernizing its own methods.

As an exile, I had occasion in 1977 to visit the FBI's New York headquarters on 69th Street and to answer questions put by "Special Agent" Ronald Hebert—questions almost identical to those put to me (just as politely) four years earlier by KGB Agent Anton Sem-yonovich at KGB headquarters on Moscow's Dzerzhinsky Street. Not being a radical and not belonging to any party, I am, as always, the inquisitive foreign writer who pokes his nose into everything and evidently is equally doted upon by his new Big Brother. Over the years, the FBI has questioned dozens of my acquaintances about me. Recently, I was mistakenly (but with great honor) called "Lermon-tov," instead of "Limonov": "So how is your friend Lermontov doing in Paris?" an FBI agent asked my friend Gennady Gum (in Russian) . . . and then blushed when he realized his mistake.

[7] Every country has its own customs, and these determine the interpretation of events that occur in the exile's life. On the evening of January 26, 1981, in Paris, the automobile in which I was riding (on the back seat) was shot up by some poorly dressed persons. Directed, at the end of a revolver barrel, to get out of the car, I learned that I had been arrested by the French police. It turned out that the local fuzz had taken to dressing up in filthy clothes and shooting at cars which ran red lights. I remember being released to the Parisian sidewalk after eighteen hours behind bars, alive, in one piece, happy, and thinking what an incredible hullabaloo would have been raised in the Western press if the Moscow police had fired on the car of a foreign or dissident writer!

Later, in 1981, I was in the throes of a different kind of exile—at an international literary conference in Los Angeles. When my friend Sasha Sokolov (author of the novels *School for Fools* and *Between the Dog and the Wolf*) checked into the Hilton, where they put up conference participants, he was handed his own room key together with a note from FBI agents who wanted to talk to him. The conversation took place the next day and lasted several hours. Among other things, the agents confided to Sokolov that they were investigating the cases of five Soviet émigrés who had married engineers from Silicon Valley (very suspicious) and, in addition, my case. After the meeting Soko-lov complained to *Washington Post* correspondent Bob Kaiser, who was at the conference, and asked him to mention the unpleasant episode in his paper. True to his word, Kaiser mentioned Sokolov's interrogation in a May 18 article. But a few weeks later the same two agents phoned Sokolov, who was living at the time in the California city of Pacific Grove, and asked him for a second meeting. It was a friendly request. In American exile, freedom of the press does not mean unfreedom for the FBI. An American citizen has the right to demand his FBI dossier through the court. Usually, he receives it several years later with many names and lines blackened out. But he does not have the right to demand that no dossier be compiled about him in the first place. The FBI even had a dossier on Hemingway.

[8]   I recently became a French citizen, having existed for thirteen years as an *apatride*. While not unpleasant, it's awkward not to have citizenship. For some reason I received my American residency papers after five and a half years, instead of the customary two. But then I keep forgetting that I am a nasty foreigner and that I write books whose action takes place in America.

July 29, 1983, was the official publication date of the English translation of my long-suffering novel *It's me—Eddie*, published by Random House. On July 26, the New York office of the Immigration and Naturalization Service (INS) issued me a new reentry permit—No. 1037378—to replace the old one, which was no longer valid. In this curious document the official stamp was placed . . . beside my photograph, rather than overlapping it. Anyone could have taken such a document and affixed his own picture to it. A half year earlier I had seen a similarly unusual document in the hands of another "bad Russian"—Valentin Prusakov, a journalist and author of the book *Neither the USSR, Nor the USA*. Before leaving the INS office, I pointed out the improper stamp in the passport and asked that my reentry permit be given an authentic appearance. "We won't change anything. The permit is entirely proper. Take it or leave it." So I took it; I had to fly to Paris.

As might have been expected, on August 2, in Charles de Gaulle Airport, a young customs official with braids on his shoulder noticed the strange appearance of my passport. I was asked to step out of line and, justifiably, taken to an inner room. There, only thanks to two other more detailed I.D.s, I was able to prove that I was who I purported to be. I was told to be sure to visit the U.S. Consulate to have my reentry permit put in order. When I went to the consulate, my request was denied. Permit me to quote, literally, the words of the refusal, as contained in a letter from Consul Caroline Higgens to the Publishing House "Ramsay": "The Embassy contacted the Immigration and Naturalization Service (INS) in Frankfurt, Germany, about

Mr. Limonov's Reentry permit. We were advised that we could make no alterations or changes to the permit, and that Mr. Limonov would have to resolve the matter with INS in New York."

The passportless exile has to have a heightened sense of humor. I do. After that, however, I had no further desire to return to the United States of America. I was afraid that the Immigration Service would confiscate my reentry permit No. 1037378 and take as long as they liked to issue me a new one, and that I would thus have to remain in the U.S.A. against my will. Any sort of pretext would do, such as, for example, a "lost" folder. It is entirely possible that I was issued this improper reentry permit with precisely this purpose in mind (as well as a fully understandable desire to make my life more complicated). I swear by the heavens that I have never been arrested in the United States, never been mentally ill, and never been a member of the hated Communist Party. Nor do I suffer from a persecution complex. For a long while I lived in France with my "false" document, and was even obliged to turn down an invitation from the Bert Bakker Publishing House to visit Holland. On another occasion I refused to travel to England when my book was published by Picador.

[9]   As you can see, all this hindered me in moving about the planet before I received French citizenship, but no one ever interfered with my writing. Both in Moscow and in New York I followed my own inclinations. As for politics, political parties, and politicians, I have always viewed them as a cancer on the body of humankind.

I cannot make the unqualified statement that I did not enjoy freedom to publish in the USSR. Before 1973 I never made any really serious attempts. Inasmuch as my verse manner is marked by an intentional primitivism (in Russian poetry I am the equivalent of Customs House Official Rousseau), I always took it for granted that my poetic production would not be to the taste of Soviet publishing enterprises and would be rejected. In 1974, however, to my amazement, the magazine *Smena* accepted for publication several of my poems. Only my departure from the USSR that same year prevented their publication.

Now that nine of my books have appeared in French translation and my first novel has even been published in half a dozen languages, I believe I have the right to consider myself a successful writer.

I have now lived for several years exclusively on income from literature. True, the majority of French and American writers would find it impossible to exist on the more than modest sums that literature provides me, but their needs are greater than mine. After twenty years of all sorts of odd jobs (tailor, stockman, steel worker, bookseller, stone mason, common laborer, painter, butler, etc.) in the USSR and the U.S.A. I am happy to have the opportunity to be just a writer.

[10]   "How do you like the French?" my Russian and American friends now ask me. I don't see that this question has any meaning. I pick my friends and acquaintances, and—as a rule—their national peculiarities are not their most important qualities. In Paris I found the same number of lunatics, and I need lunatics, as I found in Moscow or in New York. My French friends are just as unusual and unique, in their own way, as my American or Russian friends. As for the crowd on the street, all I require of it is that it does not attack me.

[11]   I neither like nor respect Soviet dissidents, any more than I liked Party and Union types in the USSR. Motivated by usually selfish or vengeful interests, the dissidents stir up public opinion and Western governments against the USSR. The second cold war has been, in many ways, the fruit of the efforts of the dissidents and their rhetoric, which is rich in phrases like "the blood-drenched Soviet regime." To curry maximum sympathy in the West, dissidents—like fishermen and hunters—have considerably dramatized their own tales of woe. Since the sixties, for example, I have been watching the number of people estimated to have perished in the camps grow steadily. Khrushchev spoke of thousands; the dissidents at the time spoke of hundreds of thousands. Now they claim the astronomical figure of seventy million! Historians cannot agree on the number of casualties in World War I (there are about a hundred estimates!), but the dissidents throw around figures in the millions, using their own vengeful emotions and masochistic ecstasy as their source. Their statement, "Our former homeland is the absolute worst!" is another Russian claim to distinction—though in reverse.

The Gulag has long ago entered into the tragic pages of Russian history, but a good two-thirds of the world—most of the countries of Latin America, Asia and Africa—are now undoubtedly trampling human rights far more energetically than their colleagues in the USSR. Nevertheless, thanks to the efforts of Soviet dissidents, the USSR has retained position No. 1 throughout the world. Alas, this is not all so innocent.

Unfortunately, I have no choice but to share exile with the dissidents, and to struggle as a writer for my place in the sun—and it is a struggle to find publishers and readers. Former Soviet writers, who cannot conceive of themselves without a boss, have managed to slip into the sphere of ideological service in their new homelands. Vladimir Maksimov, Vladimir Voinovich, Anatoly Gladilin, Georgy Vladimov, Vasily Aksyonov, and numerous other more minor figures diligently serve their new masters in radio broadcasting, cascading propaganda over the entire Soviet Union, and also in émigré newspapers and magazines—once financed directly by the CIA, but now by the U.S. State Department. From time to time these dissidents are permitted in the *Washington Post, Newsweek, Time,* etc., to beat their breasts in public paroxysms of loyalty to the new order. In exchange for their good conduct they earn such epithets as "outstanding," "major," and "famous." Right from their first visits to the West, they have managed to establish excellent contacts. For example, when Patricia Blake, an editor for *Time,* wrote a survey of Russian literature, the most important Russian writer was not Solzhenitsyn or Sinyavsky-Terts, but . . . Vasily Aksyonov. Unfortunately, *Time* readers do not suspect that Patricia Blake is a personal friend of Aksyonov and his wife.

I want to note here that the profession of dissident in the USSR has long since ceased to be that of a sapper, who errs only once. Neither Maksimov, Nekrasov, Gladilin, Vladimov, or Aksyonov ever spent a day in prison. After celebrating their departure by an expensive drunken party in a Soviet restaurant, the very next day they celebrated their arrival in the West with an expensive drunken party in a restaurant in London, Paris, New York, or (at the very least) in Vienna. "How is it your dissidents feel no shame in posing as martyrs?" the reader will exclaim. And he'll be right.

[13]   The reader must by now have realized that I am a mean person. This meanness explains precisely why I prefer to live among the quiet, nice peoples of the world. Unfortunately, there are fewer and

fewer of these quiet, nice peoples, and more and more of the nasty variety. The Armenians started killing Turks because, at the turn of the century, the Turks had butchered them. Evidently, the Jews and the Arabs will never stop killing each other. The Salvadorans are real artists at assassinating each other, while the Afghans slaughter each other and the Russians who came to their mountainous land to kill the bad Afghans. The Americans, a very civilized nation, permitted 250 of their soldiers to be killed in Lebanon. Then, to compensate for their loss, they landed in Granada, knocked off a few Granadians and Cubans, and—proud of themselves—left. The English sated their inflamed national pride by killing hundreds of Argentineans at the other end of the world, and that during bad weather.

On Rue des Rosiers, just a block away, in the Goldenberg Restaurant, they killed six people, and on my street—Rue des Ecouffes—brawling increases all the time. If Le Pen, who doesn't like foreigners, comes to power in France, I will flee into exile again. But to where?

Horst Bienek   I would like to comment on Limonov's remarks, some though not most of which I agree with. While I personally found the subject fascinating, I think it would be best not to dwell on the internal quarrels of the Russian émigrés and dissidents. I am well aware that the most mortal enemy of a Russian exile is another Russian exile, but we are here to discuss the *general* problems of exile. We have among us Rumanians, a Turk, and even a token woman, and we should keep to our main topic, and not be distracted by internal Russian frictions, which are fully capable of swallowing up all of our attention. It's not that I want to strangle the exchange of experience, but I would like to keep it within certain bounds.

Nedim Gürsel

Words of Exile

———

I am happy to have the chance to speak as a Turkish writer, since we have not yet heard much from the Middle East. The majority of writers here seem to be from the countries of the East [i.e., Eastern Europe], and a gathering like this fully justifies their presence. I, however, come from the only Islamic country that is about to request admittance to the European Community.

I write in a so-called "rare" language, which (with its dialects) is nevertheless spoken by two hundred million people, but that is not the topic I wish to broach today. Here in Vienna, a city twice besieged by my ancestors, I have decided to speak to you of my personal state of siege.

I became an exile after the coup d'état of September 12, 1980, when two of my books were seized. For ten years now I have continued to write in Turkish while living in France; thus I am besieged by the French language. For me language is clearly the central problem in our condition as writers.

But I do not want to speak to you only of writing, but also of reading, because for me, the two activities are one.

Writing is, to me, a way of life, but it is also an experience that isolates. The blank page demands solitude—that terrible meditation under the solitary splendor of a lamp that made Mallarmé giddy. He was able to meet the challenge only by setting the lamp aside. "You cannot write brightly against a dark background," he said. Kafka, who was "nothing but literature" (his own words), told Felicia of a unique project of his. He wanted to sit in the depths of a huge cave with a lamp to write by. "One is never properly alone when writing," he said. "There is never enough silence around us, and the night is never night enough."

Although I have lived in Paris for over ten years now, I have the feeling that I am living in a cave where Kafka's lamp is always lit. The truth is, I do not live in a city or in a country. I inhabit a language. Turkish is the cave, where I live like a stone in the fruit. Still, even though writing my mother tongue reassures me, I am nonetheless thwarted in my daily life by the French language, which haunts me. Sometimes it tries to break through the walls of my cave, releasing an irreversible mechanism into my writing. I am no longer able to master the rules of my own language. The French language, that ultimate place of exile, is beginning to structure my phrases. Although I continue to write in Turkish, my syntax is being distorted. To resist the impact of the present which this daily practice of French unleashes in me, I must bind myself to the words of my childhood. In describing this painful yet enriching experience, I want to show how reality can sometimes sustain the literary language without being reflected by it.

Famine in Ethiopia had a similar effect on me. I knew that this tragedy, seen in the media, could not have a direct impact on my writing. It became a commonplace tragedy, at once pervading and yet far away. Those little heads, those huge-eyed hungry children, those empty stomachs, will forever inhabit my cave, push aside my lamp and torment my memory. Their cries in the silence will remind me of the horror of an inarticulate language which is only heard, not written down. My body cannot feel the agonies suffered by the emaciated bodies of the African children, nor can it feel the agonies of those Turkish youngsters of my generation who died in prisons during a hunger strike.

Television did not show the agony of those prisoners, because the official press did not cover it, but their deaths burn in me like a spot scorched by the sun of my country. These atrocities undermine my writing, just as the French language undermines my syntax and stirs in me a kind of sacred hunger for Turkish words. Yet Sartre said that in comparison with a starving child's hunger, no book in the world has any meaning. What then can literature do? What can I, a Turkish writer living in France, do when infant deaths weigh on my conscience, as exile weighs on language? One writes with words, not with his conscience, and words have never fed anybody. So what's to be done, then? We must continue to write without confusing the pen with the sword.

"Now I know our incapacity," Sartre wrote in *Les mots*, referring to writers who wanted to be politically committed. "But never mind, I shall continue to write books; they are needed." Famine decimates disinherited populations and the desert advances further each day. We must write, even though we can't describe the desert's advance.

But writing is not enough; one must also read, because, even though it has no influence on reality, a book may contain a whole world. This was my experience, at least during childhood. As the eye scans black symbols on white pages, space widens; the doors of houses, the gates of cities, whole lives begin to open; people reveal themselves. The streets, the flickering lights of lamps, the sea, its algae, its fish, its boats, the sound of a flower's petals opening, of a bird flying, memories, mysterious packages, all, all can be contained in a book. The face of a person dying, of an old man, of a newborn babe, of a woman making love, the breathing of persons distressed, of people laughing, of the needy, the roads, the trees, the seasons can fill a book. From reading, one can learn about fires, about destruction, about growth, about the changing cities, about the setting of the sun and about songs, about the remoteness of stars, the immensity of oceans, the price of the earth, cold at night, hot during the day, with all the varieties of trees, of flowers, of mountains; the flow of water, and in the earth, all kinds of roots, insects, liquids, rocks. In books you find beings at their birth, at their deaths, at grips with love, with war, with adversity; as well as beautiful, very beautiful women. You need only to reach out your hand for a book to be able to forget . . . and to remember.

I remember that my mother read only the Koran, going through it without understanding it. As her lips moved, the words dripped from her mouth. A trickle of water dripped down, hitting the gravel: "Bismillahirrahmanirrahim. Elhamdulillah rabbil alemin." To read like that is not to grab at the universe, but to give oneself up to the flow of a voice unknown, to withdraw from objects, from the world, to melt into the warmth of a familiar body and to abandon oneself. At those moments, black signs arranged in lines on a white sheet give meaning to nothing. A voice that will say to you, "Don't be afraid, it's me!" is all you need to understand the world and to identify forms and colors. Characters do not exist. They are only the outpourings of a murmuring voice.

Far from that voice, which is soon dead and far from my mother tongue, I endeavor, now, to find again what I almost lost: my words.

Richard Kim   I'm originally from North Korea, but have lived long enough in the United States for something there to have rubbed off on me. Like most Americans, I am rather inarticulate. So let me just say a few last words today.

This morning I was totally lost. I could not quite cope with the style, the language, the rhetoric. I'll try to do better tomorrow. This afternoon I was having trouble getting excited about some of the things being said.

Now, for me to get excited about a problem or issue, it has to be something very important, maybe eternal.

So let me see if I've got this straight. To begin with, it seems to be taken for granted that all of us here are writers—a proposition I sometimes question where I myself am concerned. But let's take for granted that we are all writers. If one is going to take oneself for granted, and call oneself a writer, then I suppose one must write. I think I got that straight. To write, you need a language to write in, to write with. And I got that straight too. What, then, about this particular group that seems to have a problem selecting a language? A foreign language! A language other than one's own! Well, that's very difficult, but I think it's what's more or less taken for granted here. I had to learn Chinese, Korean, Japanese, and then English, and at that point, I said to hell with it. I am not going to study any more foreign languages. For some people it may be very easy to learn a foreign language, for others it may be totally impossible. It is simply a matter of linguistic talent and affinity. So I don't know if that is really a universal problem.

So I was a little confused there. If one has such difficulty learning a new language, then why not continue to write in one's own language? I got that straight. That brings me to a further problem: the work has to be translated. Then you ask, why bother to translate something you wrote in your own language? Well, obviously, to get it published. Then the question is, why get it published? Now that's a problem. I think I got that straight too. So that means there must be a need to be published. That's simple. You can always get published in your own language. There shouldn't be too much of a problem there. But that is not the solution. I got that straight. The work must be translated or written in another language, and then published—I assume for a wider recognition. After that the question is, why the recognition? That's one I'm going to have to sleep over.

But let me get back to the language problem. Having two children who think that they are hundred percent American, I personally can't get too excited about language. After I die, it isn't going to be a problem. It won't be any problem for my children, or for their children, grandchildren, etc. So why are we so excited about a problem that is very soon going to be over? But eventually I think I got that straight too.

Let's get back to the question of having to write and having to be published, but also of needing to achieve wider recognition, etc. Why do we take for granted that we must write? That is the problem I have to work on. It is one I have struggled with all my life. Why bother to write, for heavens' sake? Once I have decided I am going to write, the next question is what am I going to write about? But that's a second question. First I must answer the one, why bother to write at all?

There must be some tremendous sense of self-importance for someone to assume he is a writer. Where do we get this sense of self-importance? Frankly, I cannot get overly excited about this problem. If we recognize that we are not all that important, then the problem disappears. So what are we really dealing with?

Nuruddin Farah A point on language: I seem to represent a total minority, in that I was born in the oral tradition. The move from an oral tradition to a written tradition is itself one form of exile. A second point: English—the language in which I write—is my fourth language. Is it language that is so important, or the ideas contained therein? The important thing in the writer is his fire, the flame of his ideas. An editor can clean up a stylistically flawed book, making it a better book than one written by someone who is extremely articulate but basically void of ideas.

Nuruddin Farah

In Praise of Exile

When I was younger and of
a more romantic cast of mind, I had a love affair with the Somali
language, whose orthography was then no older than an infant with
teething troubles. Alas, the affair didn't last long. I had been in the
Soviet Union, touring that enormous country as a guest of the Writers' Union, while my novel was being published in weekly install-
ments by the daily newspaper in Mogadiscio. The paper's editor
received a telephone call from a member of the censorship board,
who told him to discontinue publication. When I was informed of
this turn of events by an official of the Somali Embassy in Moscow,
the news didn't disturb me. Rather, I was pleased, although at the
time I had no idea why.

Infused with unprecedented calm and self-confidence, I made a
number of unnecessary stopovers, like those of the mythical chame-
leon in the African story of creation. I gave myself a week in Buda-
pest, another in Cairo. When I flew into Somalia, I was pregnant with
ideas for the novel which was to become, in Somalia, my most well-
known work—*Sweet & Sour Milk*.

I should mention that by then I had published a number of short
stories, plays, a novella, and *From a Crooked Rib* (in English). I had
just completed my second novel, *A Naked Needle*, and posted it to
my publishers in London. The result of all this was that I told friends
and acquaintances that my novel in Somali was of no relevance to the

political changes taking place in the country (a statement with which the pro- and anti-Siyad Barre factions agreed). Abandoning it altogether, I got down to *Sweet & Sour Milk*.

Except for *A Naked Needle* (which, I am pleased to say, is out of print), all my major writing has taken place outside Somalia, beginning with *From a Crooked Rib*, which I wrote when I was a second-year student at a university in India. For me, distance distills; ideas become clearer and better worth pursuing. I like to place an intellectual and a physical distance between myself and what I am writing. By writing several drafts of a novel, and not publishing it directly, I have sought to achieve the distance which I so badly need. Withdrawals from the humdrum of everyday obsessions, anthropological reality, and self-isolations enable me to extract from life's mundanities the essence of a graphic narrative. Indeed, I did my first published effort, a novella, while hospitalized in 1965, recovering from an operation I thought I wouldn't survive. Alone in a private ward and away from home, I felt grown-up, a man endowed with a voice seeking articulation.

We Somalis are a loving lot and we are a physical people; we touch noisily, and we talk a great deal. Myself, I have a morbid dislike of crowds and loathe coming into bodily contact with more than one person at a time. My attention span, when someone else is speaking, is of a brief duration. In the years I lived in Somalia, I remember agonizing over my privacy and avoiding friends and relations who wished to talk and talk and talk.

While writing *A Naked Needle* and doing occasional pieces for the newspapers, I had no place of my own—not even a room in the family home. I discovered that you couldn't plot the overthrow of a tyrannical regime from your mother's home—a home crowded with elder brothers and younger sisters.

One of the pleasures of living away from home is that you become the master of your destiny, you avoid the constraints and limitations of your past and, if need be, create an alternative life for yourself. That way everybody else becomes *the other*, and you the center of the universe. You are a community when you are away from home—the communal mind, remembering. Memory is active when you are in exile, and it calls at the most awkward hour, like a baby waking its parents at the crack of dawn.

Before my ninth year, I was conscious of a gulf existing between myself and my parents, a gulf as wide as the distance separating the oral and written traditions, the one theirs, the other mine. For my parents the written word had a magic relevance on a par with the Holy Scriptures. And so, when the proofs of *Crooked Rib* arrived and I showed them to my mother, there was a dubious mixture of excessive delight and sadness in her eyes. One of my sisters narrated to my mother Ebla's story, translating it into Somali. My mother's reaction was: "But this happens every day, and Ebla's life is as common as sandstorms in Mogadiscio." In retrospect, I can only conclude that to her the ordinary was of no subliminal significance. The person from an oral tradition turns to the written tradition to gain access to an exalted feeling of awareness, similar to the ecstasy of a dervish chanting the Almighty's names of praise. In other words, there was no mileage in the ordinary, no magic. A writer depicting humdrum realities is comparable to a prophet incapable of performing miracles in which mountains are dislodged and rivers are turned into roads. This leads us to the notion of exile in the *Koran*.

The notion of exile is central to many faiths. In almost all of them, the prophet bearing God's message starts from a position of exile, of isolation, temptation, and meditation. The Muslim era, Hijrah, begins with the Prophet Mohammed's date of departure from Mecca. Adam's ejection, together with Eve, from paradisiac delight is where it all begins. My novels are about states of exile: about women shivering in a cruel, cold world ruled by men; about the commoner denied justice; about a torturer tortured by guilt, his own conscience; about a traitor betrayed.

However, in this prophetless age, in the Africa of inefficient dictatorships, something extraordinary, in Somali terms, occurred: I published *Sweet & Sour Milk*, a novel which made clearer, in a magical-realistic metaphor, a phenomenon known but not written about. Somalis—both those belonging to the oral and those belonging to the written traditions—began taking my works seriously, and my novel became the most talked about and read book in the country.

But I could not have written it in Somalia. For in the early days of Siyad Barre's rule, there was a great deal of applause, a noisier-than-thou clapping of hands; there was also a pronounced sense of self-adulation and self-congratulation. Since I suffer from agoraphobia, I was never part of these crowds. I spent my spare time writing. I wrote in longhand at night, only to type the same at two in the afternoon, when Mogadiscio was having its siesta. I worked in my mother's living room, tucked away from curious neighbors and the National Security paranoia.

Worried about my safety, my London publishers wouldn't release *A Naked Needle*, which I wanted published while I was still living in Somalia. In the meantime, friends, makeshift ministers in Siyad Barre's cabinet, and foreign diplomats whom I met at cocktail parties all wondered if I was writing about the "revolution." The then minister of higher education and culture (now in detention) suggested that I record the nation's historical turning point in the glowing words of a truly inspired work of fiction. I recall saying that I hadn't the time, that I had been deafened by the loudness of the applause and blinded by the dust the marchers had stirred. The minister then made an oblique reference to my novel, the publication of which had been canceled by the censors. I think he described it as "irrelevant"—to the political happenings in the country.

To "write a truly inspired work of fiction" about Somalia, I had to leave the country. If I hadn't, in all probability I would have spent many years in detention centers (prison being another form of exile). Maybe I would have been supplied with plenty of time to plot my novels, but no pens and no opportunity for publication. Maybe I wouldn't have written much; definitely my manner would not have been as confident and detached. Being away from home has provided me with the time to pursue my profession, that of a writer.

Jan Novak   I was born in Czechoslovakia, but I've lived half my life in Chicago. My first book was published in Czech, and I have now published two books in English, so I've made the transition from one language to another. I don't want to downgrade the importance of passion in a writer, but different cultures describe their worlds as people perceive them. I would imagine that Eskimos have the most words for snow, and Americans for money. When you change languages, you change your perception of the world.

My last book, which was written in English, draws on my experiences in the working world of corporate America. I work for the phone company; I run a computer operation center. The book could not have been written in Czech, because the Czech language does not have the words that this computer world uses. In fact the book was inspired by the nonsensical computer-speak of that world and its inadequacies in describing ideas and emotions. But this language has to do just that, because people have thoughts and feelings, and they wind up expressing them in this sort of corporate bureaucratese. And the product can even become a sort of skewed poetry. So language is important. That's the point I want to make.

William Gass   I would like to second that remark as a person who hasn't got the problem of many languages and who is barely able to ride the one he has. I am a little surprised by some of the remarks made today; they seem to testify to a relative ease in moving from one language to another. It would seem to me that the writer deals with specific structure and vocabulary, but the process tends to structure the very eye with which he looks at things. At any rate, I am not convinced that a person who "looks" at things in French looks at them in the same way as someone who "looks" at things in English. I have in mind the look of the written page.

My second point has to do with the music of language; without music there is no art. If you shift even your vowel sounds, you've shifted the fundamental emotional scheme of your medium, and several people have referred to the importance of that language which was the language of childhood.

Nabokov had the advantage of an English governess at an early age, and was a very great writer to boot. Nevertheless, he too frequently had to write with the top of himself, which was, of course, a highly intellectual, clever, manipulative, complex mind. And only in his memoirs did he dare to become more sentimentally human.

One of the problems that you see even in someone like Conrad, who made a shift, of course, is that he has a terrible time with women in his novels. To use an analogy which was made earlier, I suspect that he still was making love in Polish, and it was not possible to write about women the way he might have had he continued in Polish.

Now this is conjecture on my part, because I could not possibly make the step that many of you have, and therefore cannot speak for both sides. Nevertheless, the sense that I have is of the absolute

intimacy between self and language; this must be the ultimate sever-
ance, the most extraordinary violation and reorganization of the self.

I hope we will talk about the psychology of exile, and one of the
questions which I think Mr. Kim laid out (with embarrassingly beautiful logic) is the sense of importance on the part of the writer.
Perhaps Americans know this feeling even more than anybody else;
they have a feeling that nobody really cares what they say; and they
may be right. And this is, I think, something that exiled writers may
be, in a certain sense, spared. They have been carried off by
an important event and washed ashore, but let us imagine you're
washed ashore in a place like Missouri. Nobody is sitting around
waiting for your notes of beauty; they couldn't care less.

Jorge Edwards My first point is that, in general, the writer is somebody
who uses language in a different way than does the society in which
he lives. He uses language with a different meaning, with a certain
autonomy, while people in that society, as well as their institutions,
generally use language only as an instrument of direct communication. Thus the writer's real nation is his own special use of language,
and that is what is unique or eccentric. These are the roots of his
marginality in a society, and, for him, the beginning of a form of exile.

My second point is that many writers provoke their own exile in
order to improve this special relationship they have with a creative
language. In a subtle way some writers have imposed exile upon
themselves so as to create a much more intimate relationship with
their creative language. I can provide two instances.

One very special case is Joseph Conrad, who changed from Polish
to English. It seems to me that his departure from Poland was deliberately motivated by a desire to seek out an intimate relation with a
creative language. Initially, he wanted to go to France and become a
French writer, but I think the fact that he ultimately became an
English writer is of considerable significance. His father, who was a
translator of Shakespeare, had been exiled inside the Russian empire
in those days. I find it very revealing that Conrad grew up in the
house of an exile who was in constant communication with the
language of William Shakespeare.

Another case that interests me as a Chilean is that of the young
Pablo Neruda. In 1925 or 1926 Neruda asked to be sent as a consul to

the Far East. He later confessed that when he was appointed to Rangoon, he did not know where the place was and there was a hole in his map precisely where Rangoon should have been. "So," he said, "I was sent to a hole in the map." In Rangoon he wrote *Residence on Earth* (which I still believe is his best collection of verse). The title is a hidden allusion. Residence on Earth is actually residence in the language. In his letters from the Far East, he repeatedly explained that his only territory, his only certainty in those years, was the Spanish language.

Actually, his Spanish became quite odd. It was very much influenced by solitude. He heard chiefly English, as spoken in the English colonies, and his use of verbs is not altogether Chilean or Spanish. It was something new, and he made of it something very creative in the Spanish language.

All his accounts of this period, for him a very creative one, indicate anguish and anxiety, isolation, and a very critical personal state. One gets the impression that in the end Neruda (who, by the way, was a great fan of Conrad) vehemently rejected that entire part of his life, along with the poetry, and abandoned his self-imposed exile for the sake of a communitarian world. He became a Communist and a believer in the new Latin American nationalism. It was his way of fleeing the creative but very critical exile that he had imposed upon himself.

In the early years of his career, he had been, I think, very conscious of his relationship with words, and of the problem of being a member of a national community, and also of the conflict that this meant for him. When he was very young he wrote the following strange line:

> Patria, palabra triste, como termómetro, o ascensor
> (Fatherland—a sad word, like thermometer or elevator)

In this poem Neruda suggests that he sees society as a world where words are used as instruments to be manipulated for political reasons, for power. They are sad words, in contrast with the words he finds when he leaves that community for the creative isolation of exile, his residence on earth, not simply in the nation. This exile into words is my third point.

Finally, I would like to point out how the word usage of the writer who lives inside Chile differs in a revealing way from that of the writer in exile. In the last few years I have noticed that the favorite genre of Chilean exile novelists is a sort of historical-social novel intended to reexamine what happened in Chile. It is an obsessive subject among exile writers today.

Writers working inside Chile, on the other hand, favor a narrative based on the fantastic tradition of the novel. This is a narrative replete with allegorical elements and a masked alter ego invented to give the author the opportunity to speak through this invented character.

It has been suggested that this is obviously a reaction by writers "of the interior" to censorship, but I am not satisfied with this explanation. In my opinion, the problem is much more complex. Since 1981–1982 the censorship of books in Chile has not been rigorous. Over the last two or three years very few books have really been censored at all, because the dictatorship couldn't care less about fiction read by a minority. Television and the large-circulation press are censored, but not poetry and novels.

I attribute the use of the fantasy tradition to the need to manipulate, to conceal, and to use words in a slightly different way from their etymologically defined way. In our country, for instance, there is a sort of a public language that refers to authoritarian democracy and that never admits to the existence of a real censorship. We hear statements like: "We will create a society that will certainly not be a dictatorship, but neither will it be a weak democracy; it will be exactly the reverse." The reverse of what? When you find yourself in this kind of society, and are immersed in this kind of language, you tend to respond with black humor, fantasy, or allegory. The people who went into exile, on the other hand, are obsessed by the historical facts that brought about their exile. They are constantly reexamining the past—a history that ends the moment they left the country.

Nedim Gürsel In discussing, earlier, the importance of language for us writers, I said that language, not countries or cities, is our actual place of residence. I would like now to put forward a few more general reflections on language and exile.

First of all, language is not a tool, but the very object of literature. When we communicate, we employ language, but when we write, language ceases to be a simple tool and becomes the very object of our activity as writers.

Is it really possible to change one's language the way a man changes his wife? Here I address myself to my friend Tanase, who has chosen to write in French. While I respect this choice and am even tempted to write in French myself, having now lived more than ten years in France, I remain attached to my native language, to the words of my childhood. That is, I perceive an emotional connection between language and the act of writing.

Second, once a writer chooses a language that is not his mother tongue (as did Conrad and many Romanian writers, such as Tzara, Ionesco, and Cioran) there remains the problem of distance: that is, you are expressing yourself in a language with which you have no emotional tie, and you can end up disrupting this language. For example, Tzara wrote poems in French that may have been more successful than they would have been in Romanian, but they were Dadaist poems . . .

A foreign language can sometimes be imposed on the writer. In France, where the use of French is the order of the day, the Moroccan writer and Prix Goncourt laureate Tahar Ben Jelloun commented that the French language was his mistress, while the language of his mother (Arabic) was his legitimate wife. But he was happy that such a mistress was imposed on him. Evidently this situation derives from Morocco's colonial history.

A third point of interest is that of translation. I continue to write my novels in Turkish, and other people translate them into French. I often ask myself why writers are frequently incapable of translating their own books. I am bilingual and I have translated Turkish writers into French, and French writers into Turkish. Why is it then that I am incapable of translating my own books? If I were to do so, I would be tempted to rewrite the book in French; such a book would no longer be a translation. I regret the absence of translators at a gathering like the present one, because they could have brought their own testimony, their own experience. They are often better placed than we are to talk about the process of passing from one language to another.

A final point, one which also has to do with the problem of distance, but in one's own language: although I write in Turkish, the daily use of French has affected my writing. This sets an irreversible mechanism in motion; at times, it is as though I no longer knew the syntactical rules of my language. Of course, I write without committing grammatical errors, but perhaps I have lost what might be called the warmth that comes from the daily use of one's mother tongue.

Joyce too lived abroad for a long time, in a sort of exile. I wonder if it wasn't for that very reason that he became conscious of his language as a writer, and of the English language itself. Is it an accident that Joyce was so preoccupied with his language, simply as an object? He wrote books which he perhaps might not have written had he remained in Ireland.

The Spanish writer Juan Goytisolo lived in exile for many years. When, after the demise of the Franco regime, he could have returned to Spain, he chose to remain in Morocco, dividing his time between Paris and Marrakesh. He continues, however, to write in Spanish, and he tells me that it is because he was in exile that he came up with the idea of breaking through the academic and scholastic structure of the Spanish language.

This may also have happened to the majority of those among us who have opted to change languages. But can we really do that? We may become very good French writers, but we still remain, at least in part, Czech, or Spanish, or Turkish.

Antonin Liehm   Well, I believe that the one does not exclude the other, but before the money comes, the language has to be there. When Mr. Kim spoke recently, I was bursting to express my disagreement and to ask certain questions. He kept asking himself questions and saying: "I hope I got it right." And I had the feeling he got it all wrong—every time he used the phrase.

Gürsel and Edwards have already addressed the question and, I think, dispelled the misunderstanding which lay at the root of Mr. Kim's comments.

We are talking about two different things, not of language as mere communication, but of poetic language. I can speak English, or French, or German, but I am unable to create an original sentence in English or in French, except perhaps by error. We all know how important defamiliarization is in poetry. The question is: how do we defamiliarize a language with which we are not familiar?

I think Mr. Kim treated the subject somewhat lightly. People sitting around this table have struggled, sometimes traumatically, with the enormous problem which someone called the problem of the landscape, of the country in which they are living, to which they are confined. This is their language.

Another disagreement I have, of a very different kind, is with Horst Bienek, when he used the obvious examples of Nabokov and Ionesco. Are these the correct examples? Do they prove anything? Bienek says it took Nabokov twenty years to decide to write in English. But we all know these twenty years were spent in Germany. Why didn't Nabokov switch to German? He himself says that the first words he learned in life were English, and not Russian.

Ionesco was also completely bilingual as a child, and, of course, what Gürsel says is absolutely correct. Ionesco's attitude toward language is "distanced"; that's what makes Ionesco's literature possible.

There is another wonderful example—the British dramatist Tom Stoppard. Tom Stoppard, as you may or may not know, is Czech-born, but he switched languages at the age of five or six. It is the attitude toward language that remains. The unconscious part of our language, the childhood part, is gone. So do the examples of Nabokov or Ionesco really prove that a writer can switch languages?

Even in the case of Conrad there is something which should be said. Although Edwards's comments are very important, any English reader will testify that Conrad finds no difficulty when writing about the South Seas, but whenever he writes about the English countryside and English country life, you can see it is not his language. The one example I would know of and which I would more or less accept is Beckett, but Beckett creates an artificial linguistic landscape, and he needs this estrangement from the language.

What happens when the unconscious part of writing is gone or eliminated? I am not arguing that without this unconscious, no poetry, no literature is possible, but I am saying that there is a difference. When Ms. Moníková says that she was over twenty when she started writing in German, something must have been sacrificed, and something gained. But what exactly is it? I believe this question is extremely important, and not boring at all.

My other disagreement with Horst Bienek concerns his view of the Russians. The Russian language, he claims, exercises an enor-

mous spell on people writing in Russian, one they cannot rid themselves of. Russian is an obsession. I wonder why he says this. I don't
know of many American or English writers who would easily get
away from English and would start writing in another language, nor
do I know of any German writers who would do that. I think Russian
exercises the same spell as any other tongue. Why should Russian be
any different?

Richard Kim   As far as I am concerned, if I want to write, I can do so in
any way I choose, and without particularly agonizing over it. If I am
going to write something for myself, I use either Korean or English. It
is a different matter when it comes to publishing. Then the question
of language becomes important. If I were to stop writing for publication, the problem would cease to exist. I could write for myself or I
could stop writing for myself (or anybody else), and the problem
would simply cease to exist.

Horst Bienek   Permit me to respond, very briefly, to the comments of
my friend Antonin Liehm. He has not understood me correctly. I did
not mention Ionesco in this connection. His is a completely different
case.

I would like to go back to the words of our friend Mr. Virgil
Tanase. For him the shift from Romanian to French represented an
important opportunity for artistic renewal. It is crucial to realize that
the so-called "small" languages need the major languages—English,
French, German, Russian—in order to enter into world literature.

With regard to switching languages, you can learn a foreign
language well enough to communicate, but this functional skill
should not be confused with artistic expression. These are two fundamentally different phenomena. When I hear people here say that
language is no problem for them, I begin to wonder whether art itself
is no problem for them.

Jaroslav Vejvoda   First of all, I would like to turn to the social topics
mentioned by Mr. Bienek previously. I am very grateful to him for his
engagement and I would like to extend support to others who have
been affected by exile or exodus. Most people here are to some extent
privileged, but I would like to call attention to those who have not

the slightest chance of being recognized, not only as writers, but as human beings. For some of them, escape has lasted for years. I speak here of the masses of anonymous refugees who at this time of modern migration have flooded the West—"flooded" from the point of view of the so-called host countries. I say "so-called," because all Western European countries are trying to evade responsibility for these anonymous refugees who speak no foreign languages and have no lobbies. Even we exiled writers hardly notice them.

Another topic: the psychological problem of language. While doing research for a Swiss feature film dealing with modern migrations, I had occasion to talk to some Tamils. The Tamils are a people from Sri Lanka, almost all of whom are in a state of flight. I asked them about their experiences in the "host country" Switzerland. Since I do not know the Tamil language, they had to attempt to transmit their impressions to me in German. Over and over they spoke (in German) of evil persons who had driven them to flee. They spoke a very broken German which they had learned in Switzerland and constantly used the German word *also*, which means something similar to "so." This was the most hostile word that they had learned from the very proper Swiss bureaucrats. The word in and of itself has no ominous implications, but for the Tamils it had become a command, an order, perhaps even a death sentence. *Also* had become a German expression of their anxieties. They use it instead of "fire," instead of "loss," instead of "leave."

For me this was an impressive instance of the indifference which the world feels for all of us, and for all those whose anxieties find no literary expression. We must not forget these people.

I would like to give you a literary example of language psychology. The famous Swiss writer Friedrich Dürrenmatt tells the following story about a rehearsal of his play "Romulus the Great." A slave appears with the emperor's breakfast: "I bring you your breakfast," he says, using the word *Morgenessen* instead of the usual German *Frühstück*.

The actor in the leading role objected on the grounds that *Morgenessen* was Swiss dialect. Dürrenmatt, who had learned his German in Switzerland, merely smiled and broke off the rehearsal. The next day he came to rehearsal with a correction in the scene:

Slave: "I bring you your *Frühstück*."

Emperor: "Perhaps you mean *Morgenessen*?"

Slave: "The proper Latin term is *Frühstück*."

Emperor (and Dürrenmatt): "In this country I determine what is classical Latin."

That, ladies and gentlemen, is my view of the language problem.

Jaroslav Vejvoda

The Swelling Exodus

———

"I write every day just to lose myself in fictitious lives."—J. Roth to S. Zweig, 1936

"Unless it reveals an aspect of human existence hitherto unknown, a novel is immoral. The ethics of a novel have to do solely with the cognition of reality."—H. Broch, quoted from an interview with M. Kundera, Süddeutsche Zeitung, 7.10.1987

Rain in the foothills of the Alps. Persistent and acid. Pale faces behind window panes. A glittering lake, with haze on its horizon, sends out smoke signals. A lakeside town, deserted during office hours, is the setting for my reminiscences. Here I used to wait in vain for important news. Dialing phone numbers, I would receive no answer. My poor command of the language made me unintentionally offend my host, all the while remaining blissfully unaware of these offenses. Here I paid off the debts that I, a newcomer to this consumer's paradise, had initially mistaken for gifts. You can see the Town Hall where, in times of economic boom, we were given secondhand clothes and other charitable gifts. Wedged into the mountain fist, the nearby lake breathes peacefully. On its shores I used to pick up wet cigarette stubs and my first German words. There is the hotel where I learned to wash dishes so well that to this very day I reap praise from my wife. With the devotion to order of a dragoon officer in the stable, the chef used to reprove me politely.

"Have you ever heard the word 'cleanliness,' Herr Doktor?" he would say. "There is still some mustard left on this plate!"

Though clumsy, I do not break dishes any more. Everything I ever dropped here was meticulously deducted from my wages. (Only, I must admit, until I learned how to dispose of the fragments in the lake.) And it was here that I wore out my only pair of shoes, the same pair I was wearing when, with Central European lightheartedness, I did a literary waltz out of the night of my country's occupation. To be sure, the City Council bought me a pair of boots—strong, waterproof, and rather heavy for the dance floor, but very suitable for my career as a dishwasher. I did not, after all, go into exile just to dance. I use the past tense, but not because not many more refugees will be coming into my new homeland. Some cross the borders illegally—a criminal offence sometimes punishable by deportation. Of those who manage to cross the borders legally, hardly one-tenth will be granted political asylum after the constantly reduced and simplified investigation. The very legality of their journey becomes an argument for denying political asylum, since they thus fail to demonstrate a threat to their persons. It is the refugee himself who has to supply the necessary evidence. Demonstrable persecution of a political group, a *Putsch*, an occupation, or even a prison sentence for fleeing the country are not sufficient. There must have been a threat, preferably a deadly one.

What has changed in my country of adoption, in Europe, in the world? Is it the economic stability here, the political instability elsewhere? As conflict and unrest increase, the exodus to the relatively safe lands is increasing.

Edward Limonov   Can I make a bold proposal? Let's talk business; we are all professionals, not beginners, and this is not a writers' workshop. All this droning on about language doesn't interest me at all. Let's talk about money, about the publishing possibilities, let's ask if we are of any interest to the foreign reader. Let's talk about critics, about what we do, and not have another boring academic conference.

This year I published one novel in *Playboy*, and the second is to be published in December. It's the French *Playboy*, not the American, but I am very proud of it. I feel proud as a writer, because they pay well. They have large print runs, and that's what's important. So let's orient ourselves toward action . . .

Libuše Moníková   I don't necessarily consider the appearance of a text in *Playboy* to be a guarantee of its quality, even if Nabokov published there. I don't reject the possibility that such a work may be of high quality, but inclusion in *Playboy* is not the only recipe for success.

Language remains our primary problem, if only because we are introduced to society by means of a language. Even migrant workers, Tamils or others, have to come to terms with a foreign language, not on some lofty plane, but in the factories if they're lucky.

When they go out onto the street everybody who speaks to them uses the German familiar form of address—*du*. The language thus becomes a way of assessing their personal worth. Even well-intentioned German coworkers talk to them using only infinitives, as is done in commands. These *Gastarbeiters* have no chance to learn good German.

As foreigners in a foreign land we have an obligation to discuss the writer's responsibility. The greatest insults are transmitted through language.

For me it is sufficient that my name is constantly misspelled. Even intelligent, considerate people assume that they can ignore the "critical signs" instituted by Jan Hus. That bothers me. Language should be important—for all of us.

Virgil Tanase   I would like to respond to Limonov's remarks, which I find offensive.

A friend of mine was condemned to death in 1956, but was instead released many years later. In prison, he told me, there were days when he had a cigarette, and other days when he did not. He said that, although historically speaking this was just a detail, it was very important for the prisoners. As regards the equal value social systems, then, I would say to Limonov that from the historical point of view this may all amount to the same thing. But in an individual's life, which is made up of details, the difference is immense.

My second comment has to do with his publication in *Playboy*. It just so happens that I have read Limonov; it's not my fault, but I have read him. I can see why he does not have a problem with language. I wonder, though, why he uses words at all, when photos would suffice. You don't need language to take a photo, so I understand why the question of language does not particularly interest him.

Moving on to another topic, I would like to say that one should not try to transpose the genius of one's own language into another language. Likewise, any attempt to translate yourself results in a new book.

Though I have done a fair amount of translation, I have always refused to do literal translations. Incidentally, I have nothing against erotic story telling, and I freely admit that I translated "Les contes drolatiques," some thirty erotic stories by Balzac. From 500 pages of French text I ended up with 700 in Rumanian. I believe I created a new text, because the spirit of Rumanian is quite different from that of French.

Yury Miloslavsky I am a supporter of absolutely free trade. Everybody should be able to write, buy, or sell anything he wants, without asking anyone else's permission. In our exile market anyone can sell his particular goods, and the product of exile is exile, and nothing more.

Still, I am a little troubled for the customer. We have a single customer—the state, or state institutions such as the secret service, the department of propaganda, etc. It might be the terrible KGB or the lovely CIA, or the brave and beautiful Shinbeth (the Israeli secret service). At a conference at Freiburg University on recent Russian prose, I said that in the USSR, the Russian writer only had to be in touch with a single institution, the KGB. In exile, though, he has to take stock of the Soviet, American, Israeli, French, etc., secret services. But this is a personal problem of mine. I don't like governments. In fact, I hate them.

Something else bothers me. Just now everybody is talking about astonishing changes in my country. It is not Mr. Ligachev, Mr. Gorbachev, et al. who worry me so much as certain exiles in Paris, in the United States, or maybe Munich.

Wherever he is, the exile always takes the role of the conservationist. He is terribly afraid of changes in his country. By "changes" I mean changes for the good. If *perestroika* is real, people will start asking him whether he should not go back to the beginning, and start again in his native country. What they are suggesting is: "Now that there is no longer any reason for you to be in exile, wouldn't you like to get out of my home and go back to your own?" So I not only understand this question, I agree with it and await it eagerly.

Dennis Brutus   It seems to me that the question of language can be agonizing for some exiles, while for others it is an irrelevant and peripheral issue. And I think we ought to accept that reality.

Some other important questions have to do with philosophy, psychology, morality. . . . But a question which we have not discussed is the social and political significance (a) of exile in general, and (b) of the particular exile. Either this issue was self-evident, and therefore was not included in the agenda, or, alternatively, it was suppressed as perhaps too delicate and too sensitive for discussion.

It's just possible that the exile has a special social and political significance in that he or she has had the advantage of distancing himself from the problem, and of perceiving elements of the problem which are not visible to those who are too close to the situation. What I have in mind, of course, is the political situation which originally created the state of exile and brought the issue to the forefront. I am going to suggest that by distancing oneself from the specific political situation from which one was exiled, one is better able to perceive elements of possible agreement and reconciliation, and thus serve as a kind of mediator.

I recognize that this is not necessarily the obligation of the creative artist and that an audience such as this one is primarily interested in creative activity. Still, it seems to me that, even in the recognition of these potentialities, the writer can function creatively in a political and social context.

Anton Shammas   *Playboy* was mentioned here. . . . I think we all owe the ladies in this room an apology. I refer to the use of certain imagery, first by Mr. Tanase, and then by Nedim Gürsel, who likened changing languages to changing women. I find this implicitly sexist.

Secondly, Beckett, who was mentioned here, once said that a composer who is also a pianist should not compose on the piano, because if he does so, his hands will take him to places where he never intended to go. I usually use this passage from Beckett to explain why I, an Arab, write in Hebrew. If you write in your mother tongue, it's like playing the piano. You are more accurate in another language, more cautious—and perhaps more effective.

Nedim Gürsel   Yes, I would like to respond to my friend Shammas, if I had spoken in Turkish there wouldn't have been this lack of gallantry toward women, because Turkish is a language without articles. When you speak French, even the language is feminine. I take back my metaphor. It is very difficult being a Turk, because Westerners are fascinated by the Sultan's harem. However, I meant no offense. For once it is the French language which is at fault.

Anton Shammas

Exile
from a Democracy

———

Contrary to some expectations—my own included—I'd like, on this good Friday, somehow to dot the single "i" in exile and cross the two "t's" in literature, or at least one of them, from a slightly different angle. I'll be talking, for a change, about the two figures I admire most. Apparently they didn't know each other, so it's about time they made their debut together, and then I can have something to boast about. In case, rightly, you're breathless with anticipation, they are Dante and Breughel. One of them, at least, fits our discussion. It has been said of Dante that he headed the long line of Europe's banished intellectuals, and was the first to give political exile *the dignity of an institution.* "The exile given to me," he said, "I have received as an honor."

In Dante's case, some words should have been said in *praise* of exile. Let's face it: *The Divine Comedy* would never have been written if Dante had not been banished from Florence. So, in a way, we should be grateful to those who banished him. Literature, not to mention life itself, is—as you probably know—ruthless and reckless. And sometimes, perhaps not always, you must face two equally painful decisions: either to be banished from your Florence and write your Divine Comedy, or to stay home and enjoy your obscurity. There's no middle ground.

Exile for Dante proved to be very beneficial. He certainly suffered, but had he stayed home, he would have invented his own exile.

Some people, let's face it, are born to be exiled, either by a State (actual or imaginary) or by a state of mind, usually one of their own making.

Perhaps we can view Dante's case as a good refutation of Joseph Brodsky's statement, "The truth of the matter is that from a tyranny one can be exiled only to a democracy." Bear in mind that Dante was banished *from* a democracy. He was born in Florence in 1265, the year that city's Free Commune (Christian Europe's first democracy) was founded. And, if you will excuse my polite arrogance in mentioning myself in this dignified context, I come from a country which was described yesterday, in Yury Miloslavsky's wry words, as reeking of uncollected rubbish, a country sometimes referred to as Israel, otherwise as Palestine. It is the sort of democracy which can in the same week with one hand give the Jerusalem Prize for the Freedom of Man to a fine South African writer like Coetzee, and with the other hand stretched out, almost within walking distance of the acceptance speech, expel a Palestinian writer, not as fine as Mr. Coetzee perhaps, but still—a writer. Who knows, maybe one should be grateful to the state of Israel for expelling that Palestinian writer and thus giving him the opportunity to sharpen his talent on that magic whetstone known as Exile.

One last word to end this Dante business, and to try and wrap things up under today's psychological umbrella, and yesterday's lost-and-found language. It's rather a lengthy quotation, so don't regard it as a commercial break, and please stay tuned and stick around:

> We say that a certain form of speech was created by God together with the first soul. . . . In this form of speech Adam spoke; in this form of speech all of his descendants spoke until the building of the tower of Babel, which is by interpretation the Tower of Confusion; and this form of speech was inherited by the sons of Heber, who after him were called Hebrews. With them alone did it remain after the confusion, in order that our Redeemer might use, not the language of confusion, but of Grace. Hebrew, therefore, was the language which the lips of the first speaker formed.

I'm fond of using this quotation whenever I need to explain the awkward position I'm trapped in—that of an Arab who writes in Hebrew. I use this quote as a pretext and a justification, adding that the language I use to go home (I recall here Nuruddin Farah's words) is the language of Grace, and that this language of Grace—Hebrew— is the perfect language to describe my Palestinian confusion.

Exile, in a paradoxical way, leads to the invention of one's own language of Grace. For Dante this language was the Florentine vernacular in which he wrote his *Divine Comedy*, discarding the Latin, which he referred to as "the tragic style." As you probably know, that's why he called his masterpiece—written in exile, remember— *Commedia*. Here I'm afraid I must risk disagreeing with Joseph Brodsky. "If one would assign the life of an exiled writer a genre, it would have to be a tragicomedy," he declares. I see exile as a state of mind, a going *away* from the "tragic style" toward the *Commedia*, toward a personal language of Grace. It's tempting to liken my case to that of some Third World writers who call their vernacular the language of Caliban, as compared to the language of Prospero, or even, as Derek Walcott would have put it, "the language of the torturer mastered by the victim." I'd rather call it, in the words of a friend, my perfect revenge.

In case you were wondering what happened to Breughel, I haven't forgotten him. After today's session, please go to the "Kunsthistorisches Museum," second floor, room No. 10. It's a badly lit and badly arranged museum, but that will not stop your being entranced by Breughel's "Winter" painting, in the series "The Four Seasons." And, if I might make the suggestion, Nuruddin would do well to examine carefully the group of exhausted hunters in the lower left corner, and their exhausted, melancholic dogs. To recall what you said yesterday, they are on the way home. But please compare them to us exiled writers here. I'm sure this will give you all a good idea of what *real* exiles look like.

Cabrera Infante   I would like to mention something I think is unique among Spanish-speaking writers in exile, something discovered by Republican writers after their republic lost out to Franco. They realized, all at once, that there were other countries besides France and Italy. There were the countries of South America, Central America, and the Caribbean. Many writers took refuge in places like Havana, Puerto Rico, Mexico City, Buenos Aires, Caracas, etc. Among them were the poets Juan Ramón Jiménez and Luis Cernuda and the philosopher Ortega y Gasset. They discovered that they were able to go on thinking and writing in Spanish without disruption.

This is now true of other exiles, such as the Cubans who have transformed an American city called Miami into something that you might call *Havana-Bis*. Spanish is spoken everywhere in the city, Spanish books are published, Spanish newspapers are printed. Some Cubans even become impatient when they meet other Miamians— Americans—who cannot speak Spanish fluently.

This is an important phenomenon for us Spanish-speaking writers, such as Jorge Edwards, here. There is no similar opportunity for Polish, Russian, or Czech writers.

People talk about Latin America, but that's nowhere on this planet, because there is a whale of a difference between a Cuban and a Mexican, and between a Mexican and an Argentinean. The only real cohesive element is the Spanish language.

Now permit me to bring up a different topic—one which was mentioned earlier: I never chose England as a permanent place of residence. In 1966 I was forced, by the political police, to leave Spain, because they knew my past in Cuba and would not let me live in Madrid. By sheer chance I ran into a friend who wanted me to write a screenplay with him. So I went to London. It was the summer of 1966; there were young girls dancing virtually naked in the streets. There was sunshine, and I thought all this was going to last forever. But autumn came and all the naked girls wrapped themselves up in furs, and the sun disappeared (almost forever), so I was trapped there.

But something about London interested me very much—English literature and the English language. I stayed on (seemingly forever now) and translated into English two of my novels, and a book which I call *The Debunking of Cuban History*. Later I wrote a book in English called *Holy Smoke*, which has become a sort of swear word by now because of all the bans on smoking. It is a book about the relationship between the discovery of America, the discovery of smoking (which happened, funnily enough, in my home town in Cuba), and the movies. That book has so far been translated into German, French and Italian, but not into Spanish, because a certain reckless publisher paid me to translate the book myself. And I haven't been able to do it. English is such a rich language for my kind of writing, lots of puns and plays on words, paranomasia, etc., that I managed to translate only one chapter. And there the experience finished. Of course, I haven't told my publisher that the experience is finished, because I would have to give him back my advance money.

Lev Kopelev I will speak in Russian, since this is the first time for a long while that I've had the pleasant opportunity to do so.

It seems to me that, if we studied in school the era of the migration of peoples, then our grandchildren will probably study the history of the twentieth century as the history of exiles and emigrations. This century, its second half in particular, has been a time of unprecedented movement—as compared with earlier forced, artificial migrations.

Today someone mentioned Dante. He might well have spoken of Ovid, the first émigré-exile. We might discuss countries created by emigrants: the United States, Canada, the countries of Latin America. But that which has been taking place in the last decades significantly exceeds, both in quantity and quality, in essence and in character, anything that happened earlier, as when the Huguenots were expelled from France, or the Protestants from Austria. Or when the émigrés left France after the Revolution and Danton proudly said that he would remain and was prepared to go to the guillotine, because you cannot carry away your motherland on the soles of your boots. . . . But there were people who carried their motherland, if not on their boots, then in their souls and hearts.

Language is implicit in the phrase "souls and hearts." There are brilliant exceptions like Conrad and Nabokov, but they are, nevertheless, exceptions.

Our profession has now acquired a new significance. Formerly, one spoke of the "Olympians"—the great masters of the word. Today the "common laborers" of literature (such as myself)—journalists, translators, critics—have acquired their own importance. We are the *Fussvolk*—the odd-job men of literature. More than 150 years have passed since the concept of "world literature" arose. *Weltliteratur* even has its own birthday—the fifteenth of January, 1828, when Goethe first used the expression in his journal, and later employed it many times in his letters and articles. He perceived *Weltliteratur* not simply as the translation of books, but as a community of writers and translators, all working on literature.

Today this *Weltliteratur* exists, but its condition reminds one of what happened when the Tower of Babel collapsed. Frankly, we have a real mess on our hands.

In the past people, nations, and cultures knew little about each other. The first book about Russia to appear in the West was written four hundred years ago by the Austrian, Herberstein. For more than a century it remained the only one. Today we suffer from an excess of information, from a flood of literature of all kinds—books written by propagandists and agitators, misanthropic books, idealistic or demonizing books. That is why a special responsibility falls on all of us.

Events now taking place in Russia, the Ukraine, Estonia, Georgia, prove that the spiritual life of nations has always developed independently of states and political circumstances. Writers and artists can be rewarded or exiled, bought with privileges or killed. Politicians can destroy writers, as did Hitler and Stalin, Goebbels and Zhdanov. China's Cultural Revolution could rage on, but political powers cannot create poetry, or art, or culture.

As our world shrinks and the threats that hang over it become more and more palpable, all the more crucial becomes the word written by the artist in his native language and conveyed in another language by the translator.

It is my hope, in spite of all the distortions which the word "International" has undergone in combination with other words such as "Second," "Third," "Fourth," etc., that Goethe's dream will one day become reality. The word is the only instrument capable of preventing the great disaster that today threatens mankind. SDI, bunkers, and bomb shelters cannot save us. The spirit, incarnated in the word, is humanity's last hope.

Vladimir Voinovich   We seem now to have reached the theme of language in emigration. I think, however, that all the themes we have touched on, together with all the circumstances in the life of the writer in exile, are interrelated.

In general, it is difficult to be a writer—even in the country where one is born and brought up. Everything prevents a writer from working. Wealth is just as much a hindrance as is poverty. If a writer is single, he is hindered by the general disorder of his life. If he is married, his wife and children hinder him. One writer complained that it was impossible to work in his cramped apartment; later he somehow managed to become wealthy and bought himself a big house with a large piece of land. All around was wonderful countryside—forest, ravines, streams, ideal conditions. But the writer decided that he needed to redo something in his house, to put up a new fence, to build a terrace, to dig up some trees and to plant others. Then he had, of course, to gather mushrooms and berries, cut wood for the fireplace, pickle cabbage, make vodka and fruit wines. He now had no time left for writing books. A year went by, then two. The writer had not written a line. And this depressed him. His wife decided to save him; she gathered up all his tools, his spades and his rakes, and hid them. When she left for town, she made her husband promise that he would sit down and write. When she returned she did not find him in his study. She looked for him for a long time, and finally found him in the shed. He was sitting in the corner, polishing an old copper basin.

On another occasion she locked him in his office and even removed all distracting objects, including books. He had only a table, a chair, a typewriter and a stack of paper at his disposal. A few hours later, she opened the door and saw that again the writer had not written anything. "What have you been doing?" she asked. It turned out that he had been multiplying the horizontal squares on the wallpaper by the vertical.

Later he began to write again, but no longer as well as before he achieved these "ideal" conditions. Such cases are frequent among émigrés, and not only among émigrés.

I was in Paris recently and there Francis King, president of the International PEN Club, said that writers who have emigrated do not generally write as well as they had in their native countries. He said that it was not a very pleasant thing for him to say, but it was the truth. I must say, and it is equally unpleasant for me to say this, that what he said is not true. Writers emigrate not only from one country to another, but from one book to another.

There are writers of one book. The Russian story-writer Yershov, for instance, wrote a remarkable fairy tale, and his literary career thereupon ended. The Russian playwright Griboyedov wrote a brilliant play, *Woe from Wit*, but nothing he wrote afterward bears comparison. Salinger wrote and wrote, and finally produced a remarkable book. Then he also vanished into the woodwork. If any of these writers had lived abroad, people would say: "Of course: he became an émigré, and see what happened to him."

In the Soviet Union there are writers who, without ever emigrating, lose any ability they may formerly have had. Take, for example, the late Soviet novelist Mikhail Sholokhov. He never emigrated anywhere; he never even moved to Moscow. He lived in his native village his entire life. At the age of thirty-five he completed his epic novel *The Quiet Don* (a remarkable epic, if in fact he really wrote it, but that is another question). Thirty-five is young for an author, but even so he never wrote anything worthwhile again. The quality of his work kept degenerating until it reached rock bottom in his novel *They Fought for the Fatherland*. I know of no émigré author who has written anything *so* void of any merit whatsoever.

A good deal depends on the writer—the age at which he went abroad, what kind of country he left. I can understand that a writer from a small country with few potential readers might want to switch languages. But we Russian writers have an imperialist language. Russian is the language of a huge nation, and we remember that country, wherever we may be, and hope the people back there will listen to us. This awareness hinders us from switching to the language of some smaller country.

The great writer Nikolai Gogol, for example, wrote in Russian, although he was Ukrainian, and even now many Ukrainians cannot forgive him. Yet he did not write a pure Russian; it was contaminated with Ukrainianisms.

[Voice from the audience: "He enriched the language!"]

I don't agree, because no one was able to follow his example, and his personal language is a kind of miracle, an alloy of two languages.

In the Soviet Union we have Fazil Iskander writing about his native Abkhazia, but in Russian. Or there is the singer Bulat Okudzhava, whose father was Georgian, and his mother Armenian, but who writes remarkable songs in Russian. I once asked him what he was. "I am a Muscovite," he answered.

Literature is like the writer. A writer can be cosmopolitan, and a literature can also be cosmopolitan. But there is another literature, which has national roots. For example, I can imagine *Faust* written in French or English, but I cannot say the same of *Don Quixote*,

Oblomov, or *The Good Soldier Schweik*. Take Czech literature: I can imagine that Karel Čapek's *War with the Salamanders* could have been written in another language, but I cannot imagine the short story "The Poet" in any language but Czech. This matters to me when I read that story. It matters to me that it was written in Czech, although I read it in Russian. I sense the spirit of the Czech people.

A good deal, in other words, depends on the individual author. Changing to another language may benefit one person. For others this is not essential.

Horst Bienek   In a day or so we will be scattered by the winds over half the globe (the writers here are, after all, *exiles*), and I would like to see our conference result in something more than a paperback with our speeches. Would it not be better to plan some sort of event? Ms. Steinberg has suggested that instead of limiting ourselves to reading our papers, we might devote more time to discussion. We had, she said, to "work." And work involves action, so I would like to make a proposal.

I appeal here to the Wheatland Foundation, to the Getty Foundation, and to the Steinberg Foundation to establish an annual prize for a work written in exile, a work wrung from the bowels of exile.

My teacher, Bertolt Brecht, used to say that truth must be concrete, so I would like to propose the concrete sum of $100,000. [Laughter in the audience.] I will be even more concrete: I can even make nominations for the jury [more laughter]: perhaps Lord Weidenfeld as a European publisher, an American publisher, Joseph Brodsky to represent the "Eastern Block," if I may use the phrase, Guillermo Cabrera Infante for Latin America, Susan Sontag to represent the media. Perhaps we could get together as early as next year here in Vienna and award the first prize.

Edward Limonov   And the prize will again be given to Joseph Brodsky, because he has already received half the prizes of the world.

William Gass   Prize giving can be a very tempting thing. I have in mind an award to chairs of conferences . . .

Georgy Vladimov   I am afraid there is little I can add to the question of language, which we have been discussing, because I have, in a way, closed the book on this problem, at least for myself. The subject, as someone said, is deeply individual and depends very much on one's age. Around fifty you suddenly discover that you are no longer capable of mastering a foreign language well enough to make it an instrument of creativity. So you set aside that language for everyday use and try to preserve the one language you have thoroughly mastered—your own.

There are an infinite number of native languages—as many as there are writers. Tolstoy's is one, Chekhov's another, Gorky's yet a third Russian language, and so forth. We ought to try to preserve this language and not litter it with foreign expressions of all kinds, Germanisms, Anglicisms, Gallicisms. We ought to try to prevent it from becoming old-fashioned, because that destroys the tie of trust between the author and his readers in the mother country.

The point I am leading up to is that the prime task of a writer should remain to serve his people, and through this service to participate in world literature. Unfortunately, we have not yet said much about one very important problem—the relationship between an exile and his country.

We must keep in mind that it is the inconvenient writer who is the first to be exiled by the totalitarian state. There are tens of thousands of professional people—engineers, doctors, lawyers—who dream about such an event, who devote years to the struggle to leave their country, but who never achieve this right. Meanwhile, the state gladly and easily rids itself of these writers, even when it would be quite possible and desirable to clap them in prison.

What is it that encourages the state to eject an inconvenient writer? It counts on the fact that exile will destroy him. That he will be defeated by the difficult problem of adaptation, and that for a long time this will distract him from his work. The problem of adaptation is significantly more complicated for a writer than for an engineer or a doctor, who has to master a new professional terminology or a language for everyday communication. A writer has to learn the history, geography, culture, and mentality of the people among whom he is now living and working and who will, in part, give creative nourishment to his work.

There is also the danger that the writer may be forgotten in his own country. To my amazement, and to the amazement of my colleagues, this somehow has not happened. Of late, many of our Soviet colleagues have been able to come to the West and have told us that our readers have not forgotten us. What is even more interesting is that the state which exiled us has not forgotten us either. Not long ago several articles appeared in the Soviet press, in which I figured as the protagonist. These articles were full of all manner of insults and rubbish. Russian writers, however, are used to such abuse and accept it, to borrow the words of Stephen Crane, as a "red badge of courage."

Ever since Gorbachev announced his program of *glasnost* and *perestroika*, which was to a significant degree directed at the West, the state seems to have been carefully following our every step, catching each slip or mistake. They want to know what we are going to say to our Western colleagues and readers in the West.

Recently there was an unprecedented attempt at dialogue, in which ten émigré writers wrote an open letter on *perestroika*. This letter was published in the newspaper *Moskovskie novosti.* [See *New York Times*, March 22, 1987—ed.] True, the attempt at dialogue was not made in good faith, since instead of publishing the original Russian text, the Soviet authorities published a reverse translation from the French. (The language problem again.)

Be that as it may, the dialogue did take place, and I think that it will be continued, since it was followed by comments of readers— some spontaneous, some prearranged. In other words, the letter enjoyed considerable resonance among our compatriots in the Soviet Union.

The life of the exiled writer, spent as it is in unfamiliar and often difficult surroundings, is always geared to the same end, that of telling the truth to the people back home.

I will claim your attention a little longer, so as to touch on Limonov's speech, and also that of my other compatriot, Yury Miloslavsky. We should beware of becoming so engrossed in metaphysics that we ignore other more simple but extremely relevant problems. Unlike my dear friend Horst Bienek, I cannot simply wave aside Edward Limonov's speech, because while some of what he said was unjust, some of it was painfully true. I am not going to discuss his attitude toward dissidents, for whom he has expressed his dislike, or his words to the effect that the millions of political prisoners in the Soviet Union are only a myth, and so forth.

Limonov brought up a topic I would call "Russian Literature and the CIA." Having escaped the claws of one system of propaganda, the exiled writer finds himself in danger of falling into the claws of a system of counterpropaganda. Within the émigré community the suspicion has arisen that the Russian free press is, in fact, not so free after all. For some reason, the financing of Russian periodicals, or more correctly, the task of controlling this financing, has been entrusted to the CIA.

Please understand that I recognize the need for espionage and counterespionage, and I have nothing against this respectable agency. I can even reveal that I have a soft spot for Agent 007, James Bond, precisely because he does what he is supposed to do. He runs, jumps, shoots, and overcomes various obstacles, and in the course of his activities he attracts the attention of many women, an activity in which he shows excellent taste. The one thing he does not do is give instructions to writers and editors. Unfortunately, James Bond is merely Ian Fleming's splendid creation. In reality, secret service agents have long suffered from a secret passion for directing literature, which for some reason they feel better qualified to do than the writers themselves.

I have had the experience, the sad experience, of editing the Russian émigré journal *Grani*. It is not for me to judge the quality of this journal under my editorship; I can say that I attempted to make it intellectual and pluralistic. Unfortunately, however, this journal belongs to a political party which, at its inception forty years ago, had a quite different idea of what a journal intended for Russia should be like and the editor it should have.

Conflict was unavoidable, and incompatibilities became immediately apparent. But it is strange and sad that a respectable agency of democratic America should take the side of a political party in this conflict, and not my side; that is, the side of a writer recently arrived from Russia. The principle "He who pays the piper calls the tune" triumphed. I consider this principle to be unacceptable for a writer, and I reject it.

That great country, the United States of America, with its various institutions, its universities, and its charitable foundations, has done a great deal for Russian émigré writers. It has substantially helped many of them to get on their feet. Russian literature will never forget this help. But America should be proud to render such assistance and carry it out openly, perhaps through Congress or some special Senate committee, and not through the secret service. Espionage has its own tasks, and the writer his own; and they are completely different.

William Gass   Do we have any responses? Any defence of the CIA?

Edward Limonov   We like the CIA. Long live the CIA!

Sergei Dovlatov   I am from the Soviet Union; I was born in Bashkiria. My father was half-Jewish, and my mother Armenian. I now live in the German quarter of New York City. I speak, and more important, write, only in Russian. My books are translated into English by a Polish Jew. In brief, I am a more or less typical Russian émigré writer.

Before turning to my own views, I would like to add something to what Georgy Vladimov had to say, something that he could not give—an evaluation of the journal which he edited for, unfortunately, such a short time. As an author who has contributed to many, if not to all, the Russian émigré publications, I would like to say that this was the only journal to which it was a pleasure and not an insult to contribute.

Not long ago I spent three days with the well-known Leningrad poet Viktor Sosnora, who visited America at the invitation of Allen Ginsberg and Norman Mailer. I asked him what was happening in contemporary Soviet literature. "Nothing is happening," he answered. When I asked how that was possible, he responded, "Because all of you have left." "What do you mean, everyone has left?" I said. "We feel the reverse—that everyone remained behind, and that only a handful have left." Then he said: "No, no, everyone has left but me." He said that all the vital literary forces, all the best Russian writers, were now in the West. And for some time we went on in this key.

Thirty years ago Khrushchev undertook reforms in the Soviet Union which were in many respects in harmony with processes now underway. During the remaining years of his life in retirement, Khrushchev's cronies probably used to say to him, "Nikita Sergeyevich, you made a serious mistake. You underestimated the Russian intelligentsia and that cost you your job." This was the accepted view at the time.

Evidently Gorbachev, who is in many respects a successor to Khrushchev, has learned from Khrushchev's mistake. Not only has he not underestimated the Russian intelligentsia, he has actually overestimated it, or so at least it seems to me. He has provided the creative Russian intelligentsia with a limited but visible opportunity to make itself known, and to express itself.

Nevertheless, I believe Gorbachev is committing an extremely serious mistake. He has underestimated the émigrés. For some strange, incomprehensible, enigmatic and even mystical reason, the émigrés always used to seem important to the "metropole." They were a sort of *idée fixe*.

The most significant émigré to follow Kurbsky was the great Russian émigré writer and journalist Alexander Herzen, who for thirty years kept the whole of Russia in a constant state of agitation. He did this from his home in London, and he was virtually the only man whom both Lev Tolstoy and Dostoevski respected.

There was another great émigré, Vladimir Ilyich Lenin, who could in many respects be considered Herzen's successor. He pulled off nothing more nor less than the October Revolution. Furthermore, the government he formed consisted almost entirely of émigrés.

Or take the coarse and uneducated Iosif Vissarionovich Stalin. Even he had strolled down the elegant streets of Western Europe. In this way the émigrés have always played an important role in my country.

I would now like to bring all my different points together and to prophesy as to the future of the émigré community. Fulfillment of what I am about to say is so near that you will all be able to judge the accuracy of these prophecies.

I believe that if Mikhail Sergeyevich Gorbachev does not reassess the émigrés in the near future, serious problems may lie in store for him. If, on the other hand, he corrects this error, it may be possible in the near future to institute an important dialogue between the Russians living in Russia and the émigrés. We émigrés are inclined to be skeptical about this dialogue, but it has now become clear to me that this skepticism is shared, though to a much smaller degree, by those living in Russia.

Conducted with intelligence, dignity, tact and honor (and without vanity), this dialogue may provide Russian writing with the most responsible and serious choice in the entire span of its cultural history. If this dialogue is going to be productive, Russian writers will face the following choice: either they will give up all their respective privileges, sacrifices, torments, exiledoms, and sufferings and sit down at their desks in conditions of relative or complete freedom and create masterpieces (something which has not happened for a long time), or they will have to admit that Russian literature has lost its world significance.

Lev Kopelev   I would like to support what Georgy Vladimov said here. He spoke the truth—a bitter truth, and one, unfortunately, little known in the German-speaking countries, or in America.

I would like to stress that the people who have either fled from the East to the West or have been forced to come here did so in search of freedom. Sadly, not all of them have succeeded in finding that freedom. Many here compromise themselves and choose a sort of thraldom. Vladimov made a bold attempt to be a free writer and the free editor of a free journal. I read this journal carefully, and I can say that the ten issues which he put out were truly a fine, pluralistic accomplishment, unburdened by ideological limitations. That labor could and should have been continued. He was prevented from carrying on his work by a specific governmental organization. I have no particular sympathies for James Bond or for any secret services, be they red, black, green, or checkered. The worst thing these secret agencies can get up to is tamper with culture and take over the management of literature and art.

For this reason I support Vladimov's speech and ask that my colleagues, together with the ladies and gentlemen who invited us here and who exercise considerable influence in the great land of America, weigh his words and take our pressing needs into consideration.

You can help us: you have the money, you have the influence, you are free. Help us to be free, free to create and conduct an unfettered dialogue with our kinsmen on the other side of the border—without any political interference and independent of all secret services. That will help everybody, not just us.

Jiří Gruša   I would like to put a question to Mr. Vladimov, whose work I value highly.

I was taken aback by a phrase you used, *sluzhenie narodu*, which means "to serve the people." Do you really see this as the task of literature? For me this definition is linked to those things which for decades and even centuries have forced us writers to go into exile. According to this definition of literature, there is some lofty institution which we are obligated to serve. My question is: did I understand you correctly? And if so, is this merely an empty turn of phrase or is this a deep-lying Russian attitude?

Georgy Vladimov   It may be that my phrase arises precisely from that tradition in Russian literature which has always placed service to the people above all else. I mean service to the *Russian* people. Only thus can it enter and participate in world literature. Is that clear enough?

Joseph Brodsky

*The Condition We
Call "Exile"*

━━━━━━━

As we gather here, in this
attractive and well-lit room, on this cold December evening, to discuss the plight of the writer in exile, let us pause for a minute and
think of some of those who, quite naturally, didn't make it to this
room. Let us imagine, for instance, Turkish *Gastarbeiters* prowling
the streets of West Germany, uncomprehending or envious of the
surrounding reality. Or let us imagine Vietnamese boat people bob-
bing on high seas or already settled somewhere in the Australian
outback. Let us imagine Mexican wetbacks crawling the ravines of
southern California, past the border controls into the territory of the
United States. Or let us imagine shiploads of Pakistanis disembark-
ing somewhere in Kuwait or Saudi Arabia, hungry for menial jobs the
oil-rich locals won't do. Let us imagine multitudes of Ethiopians
trekking some desert on foot into Somalia (or is it the other way
around?), escaping the famine. Well, we may stop here because that
minute of imagining has already passed, although a lot could be
added to this list. Nobody has ever counted these people and nobody,
including the UN relief organizations, ever will: coming in millions,
they elude computation and constitute what is called—for want of a
better term or a higher degree of compassion—migration.

Whatever the proper name for this phenomenon is, whatever the
motives, origins, and destinations of these people are, whatever their
impact on the societies which they abandon and to which they come,

one thing is absolutely clear: they make it very difficult to talk with a straight face about the plight of the writer in exile.

Yet talk we must; and not only because literature, like poverty, is known for taking care of its own kind, but more because of the ancient and perhaps as yet unfounded belief that, were the masters of this world better read, the mismanagement and grief that makes millions hit the road could be somewhat reduced. Since there is not much on which to rest our hopes for a better world, and since everything else seems to fail one way or another, we must somehow maintain that literature is the only form of moral insurance that a society has; that it is the permanent antidote to the dog-eat-dog principle; that it provides the best argument against any sort of bulldozer-type mass solution—if only because human diversity is literature's lock and stock, as well as its raison d'être. We must talk because we must insist that literature is the greatest—surely greater than any creed—teacher of human subtlety, and that by interfering with literature's natural existence and with people's ability to learn literature's lessons, a society reduces its own potential, slows down the pace of its evolution, ultimately, perhaps, puts its own fabric in peril. If this means that we must talk to ourselves, so much the better: not for ourselves but perhaps for literature.

Whether he likes it or not, *Gastarbeiters* and refugees of any stripe effectively pluck the orchid out of an exiled writer's lapel. Displacement and misplacement are this century's commonplace. And what our exiled writer has in common with a *Gastarbeiter* or a political refugee is that in either case a man is running away from the worse toward the better. The truth of the matter is that from a tyranny one can be exiled only to a democracy. For good old exile ain't what it used to be. It isn't leaving civilized Rome for savage Sarmatia anymore, nor is it sending a man from, say, Bulgaria to China. No, as a rule what takes place is a transition from a political and economic backwater to an industrially advanced society with the latest word on individual liberty on its lips. And it must be added that perhaps taking this route is for an exiled writer, in many ways, like going home—because he gets closer to the seat of the ideals which inspired him all along.

If one were to assign the life of an exiled writer a genre, it would have to be tragicomedy. Because of his previous incarnation, he is capable of appreciating the social and material advantages of democracy far more intensely than its natives do. Yet for precisely the same reason (whose main by-product is the linguistic barrier), he finds himself totally unable to play any meaningful role in his new society. The democracy into which he has arrived provides him with physical safety but renders him socially insignificant. And the lack of significance is what no writer, exile or not, can take.

For it is the quest for significance that very often constitutes the rest of his career. To say the least, it is very often a literary career's consequence. In the case of the exiled writer, it is almost invariably the cause of his exile. And one is terribly tempted to add here that the existence of this desire in a writer is a conditioned response on his part to the vertical structure of his original society. (For a writer living in a free society, the presence of this desire bespeaks the atavistic memory every democracy has of its unconstitutional past.)

In this respect, the plight of an exiled writer is indeed much worse than that of a *Gastarbeiter* or the average refugee. His appetite for recognition makes him restless and oblivious to the superiority of his income as a college teacher, lecturer, small magazine editor or just a contributor—for these are the most frequent occupations of exiled authors nowadays—over the wages of somebody doing menial work. That is, our man is a little bit corrupt, almost by definition. But then the sight of a writer rejoicing in insignificance, in being left alone, in anonymity is about as rare as that of a cockatoo at the Polar Circle, even under the best possible circumstances. Among exiled writers, this attitude is almost totally absent. At least, it is absent in this room. Understandably so, of course, but saddening nonetheless.

It is saddening because if there is anything good about exile, it is that it teaches one humility. One can even take it a step further and suggest that the exile's is the ultimate lesson in that virtue. And that it is especially priceless for a writer because it gives him the longest possible perspective. "And thou art far in humanity," as Keats said. To be lost in mankind, in the crowd—crowd?—among billions; to become a needle in that proverbial haystack—but a needle someone is searching for—that's what exile is all about. Lay aside your vanity, it says, you are but a grain of sand in the desert. Measure yourself not against your pen-pals but against human infinity: it is about as bad as the inhuman one. Out of that you should speak, not out of your envy or ambition.

Needless to say, this call goes unheeded. Somehow a commentator on life prefers his position to his subject and, when in exile, considers it grim enough not to aggravate it any further. As for such appeals, he considers them inappropriate. He may be right, although calls for humility are always timely. For the other truth of the matter is that exile is a metaphysical condition. At least, it has a very strong, very clear metaphysical condition; to ignore or to dodge it is to cheat yourself out of the meaning of what has happened to you, to doom yourself into remaining forever at the receiving end of things, to ossify into an uncomprehending victim.

It is because of the absence of good examples that one cannot describe an alternative conduct (although Czesław Miłosz and Robert Musil come to mind). Maybe just as well, because we are here evidently to talk about the reality of exile, not about its potential. And the reality of it consists of an exiled writer constantly fighting and conspiring to restore his significance, his leading role, his authority. His main consideration, of course, is the folks back home; but he also wants to rule the roost in the malicious village of his fellow émigrés. Playing ostrich to the metaphysics of his situation, he concentrates on the immediate and tangible. This means besmirching colleagues in a similar predicament, bilious polemics with rival publications, innumerable interviews for the BBC, Deutsche Welle, ORTF [French Radio-Television] and The Voice of America, open letters, statements for the press, going to conferences—you name it. The energy previously spent in food lines or petty officials' musty anterooms is now released and gone rampant. Unchecked by anyone, let alone his kin (for he is himself now a Caesar's wife, as it were, and beyond suspicion—how could his maybe-even-literate-but-aging spouse correct or contradict her certified martyr?), his ego grows rapidly in diameter and eventually, filled with CO_2, lifts him from reality—especially if he resides in Paris, where the Mongolfière brothers set the precedent.

Traveling by balloon is precipitous and, above all, unpredictable: too easily one becomes a plaything of the winds, in this case, political winds. Small wonder then that our navigator keenly listens to all the forecasts, and on occasion ventures to predict the weather himself. That is, not the weather of wherever he starts or finds himself en route, but the weather at his destination, for our balloonist is invariably homeward bound.

And perhaps the third truth of the matter is that a writer in exile is, by and large, a retrospective and retroactive being. In other words, retrospection plays an excessive (compared with other people's lives) role in his existence, overshadowing his reality and dimming the future into something thicker than its usual pea soup. Like the false prophets of Dante's *Inferno*, his head is forever turned backward and his tears, or saliva, are running down between his shoulder blades. Whether or not he is of elegiac disposition by nature is beside the point: doomed to a limited audience abroad, he cannot help pining for the multitudes, real or imagined, left behind. Just as the former fill him with venom, the latter fuel his fantasy. Even having gained the freedom to travel, even having actually done some traveling, he will stick in his writing to the familiar material of his past, producing, as it were, sequels to his previous works. Approached on this subject, an exiled writer will most likely evoke Ovid's Rome, Dante's Florence, and—after a small pause—Joyce's Dublin.

Indeed, we've got a pedigree, and a much longer one than that. If we want, we can trace it all the way back to Adam. And yet we should be careful about the place it tends to occupy in the public's and our own minds. We all know what happens to many a noble family over generations, or in the course of a revolution. Family trees never make or obscure the forest; and the forest is now advancing. I am mixing metaphors here, but perhaps I can justify this by remarking that to expect for ourselves the kind of future that we constitute for the above-mentioned few is imprudent rather than immodest. Of course a writer always takes himself posthumously: and an exiled writer especially so, inspired as he is not so much by the artificial oblivion to which he is subjected by his former state, but by the way the critical profession in the free marketplace enthuses about his contemporaries. Yet one should go carefully about this type of self-estrangement, not for any other reason than a realization that, with the population explosion, literature, too, has taken on the dimensions of a demographic phenomenon. Per reader, there are simply too many writers around today. A couple of decades ago a grown man thinking about books or authors yet to be read would come up with thirty or forty names; nowadays these names will run in the thousands. Today one walks into a bookstore the way one enters a record shop. To listen to all these groups and soloists would be to overshoot a lifetime. And very few among those thousands are exiles, or even particularly good. But the public will read them, and not you, for all your halo, not because it is perverse or misguided, but because statistically it is on the side of normalcy and trash. In other words, it wants to read about itself. On any street of any city in the world at any time of night or day there are more people who haven't heard of you than those who have.

The current interest in the literature of exiles has to do, of course, with the rise of tyrannies. Herein perhaps lies our chance with the future reader, though that's the kind of insurance one would like to do without. Partly because of this noble caveat, but mainly because he can't think of the future in any other than the glowing terms of his triumphant return, an exiled writer sticks to his guns. But then why shouldn't he? Why should he try to use anything else, why should he bother probing the future in any other fashion, since it is unpredictable anyhow? The good old stuff served him well at least once: it earned him exile. And exile, after all, is a kind of success. Why not try another tack? Why not push the good old stuff around a bit more? Apart from anything else, it now constitutes ethnographic material, and that goes big with your Western, Northern, or (if you run afoul of a right-wing tyranny) even Eastern publisher. And there is always the chance of a masterpiece in covering the same turf twice, which possibility doesn't escape the eye of your publisher, either, or at least it may provide future scholars with the notion of a "myth-making" element in your work.

But however practical sounding, these factors are secondary or tertiary among those that keep an exiled writer's eyes firmly trained on his past. The main explanation lies in the aforementioned retrospective machinery that gets unwittingly triggered within an individual by the least evidence of his surroundings' strangeness. Sometimes the shape of a maple leaf is enough, and each tree has thousands of these. On an animal level, this retrospective machinery is constantly in motion in an exiled writer, nearly always unbeknownst to him. Whether pleasant or dismal, the past is always a safe territory, if only because it is already experienced; and the species' capacity to revert, to run backward—especially in its thoughts or dreams, since there we are safe as well—is extremely strong in all of us, quite irrespective of the reality we are facing. Yet this machinery has been built into us, not for cherishing or grasping the past (in the end, we don't do either), but more for delaying the arrival of the present—for, in other words, slowing down a bit the passage of time. See the fatal exclamation of Goethe's Faust.

And the whole point about our exiled writer is that he, too, like Goethe's Faust, clings to his "fair," or not so fair, "moment," not for beholding it, but for postponement of the next one. It's not that he wants to be young again; he simply doesn't want tomorrow to arrive, because he knows that it may edit what he beholds. And the more tomorrow presses him, the more obstinate he becomes. There is terrific value in this obstinacy: with luck, it may amount to intensity of concentration and then, indeed, we may get a great work of literature (the reading public and the publishers sense that, and this is why—as I've already said—they keep an eye on the literature of exiles).

More often, however, this obstinacy translates itself into the repetitiveness of nostalgia, which is, to put it bluntly, simply a failure to deal with the realities of the present or uncertainties of the future.

One can, of course, help matters somewhat by changing one's narrative manner, by making it more avant-garde, by spicing the stuff with a good measure of eroticism, violence, foul language, etc., after the fashion of our free-market colleagues. But stylistic shifts and innovations greatly depend on the condition of the literary idiom "back there," at home, the links with which have not been severed. As for the spice, a writer, exiled or not, never wants to appear to be influenced by his contemporaries. Perhaps an additional truth about the matter is that exile slows down one's stylistic evolution, that it makes a writer more conservative. Style is not so much the man as the man's nerves, and on the whole exile provides one's nerves with fewer irritants than the motherland does. This condition, it must be added, worries an exiled writer somewhat, not only because he regards existence back home as more genuine than his own (by definition, and with all attendant or imagined consequences for normal literary process), but because in his mind there exists a suspicion of a pendulum-like dependency, or ratio, between those irritants and his mother tongue.

One ends up in exile for a variety of reasons and under a number of circumstances. Some of them sound better, some worse, but the difference has already ceased to matter by the time one reads an obituary. On the bookshelf your place will be occupied, not by you, but by your book. And as long as they insist on making a distinction between art and life, it is better if they find your book good and your life foul than the other way around. Chances are, of course, that they won't care for either.

Life in exile, abroad, in a foreign element, is essentially a premonition of your own book-form fate, of being lost on the shelf among those with whom all you have in common is the first letter of your surname. Here you are, in some gigantic library's reading room, still open. . . . Your reader won't give a damn about how you got here. To keep yourself from getting closed and shelved you've got to tell your reader, who thinks he knows it all, about something qualitatively novel—about his world and himself. If this sounds a bit too suggestive, so be it, because suggestion is the name of the whole game anyhow, and because the distance exile puts between an author and his protagonists indeed sometimes begs for the use of astronomical or ecclesiastical figures.

This is what makes one think that "exile" is, perhaps, not the most apt term to describe the condition of a writer forced (by the state, by fear, by poverty, by boredom) to abandon his country. "Exile" covers, at best, the very moment of departure, of expulsion; what follows is both too comfortable and too autonomous to be called by this name, which so strongly suggests a comprehensible grief. The very fact of our gathering here indicates that, if we indeed have a common denominator, it lacks a name. Are we suffering the same degree of despair, ladies and gentlemen? Are we equally sundered from our public? Do we all reside in Paris? No, but what binds us is our book-like fate, the same literal and symbolic lying open on the table or the floor of the gigantic library, at various ends, to be trampled on or picked up by a mildly curious reader or—worse—by a dutiful librarian. The qualitatively novel stuff we may tell that reader about is the autonomous, spacecraft-like mentality that visits, I am sure, every one of us, but whose visitations most of our pages choose not to acknowledge.

We do this for practical reasons, as it were, or genre considerations. Because this way lies either madness or the degree of coldness associated more with the pale-faced locals than with a hot-blooded exile. The other way, however, lies—and close too—banality. All of this may sound to you like a typically Russian job of issuing guidelines for literature, while, in fact, it's simply one man's reactions to finding many an exiled author—Russian ones in the first place—on the banal side of virtue. That's a great waste, because one more truth about the condition we call exile is that it accelerates tremendously one's otherwise professional flight—or drift—into isolation, into an absolute perspective: into the condition at which all one is left with is oneself and one's language, with nobody or nothing in between. Exile brings you overnight where it would normally take a lifetime to go. If this sounds to you like a commercial, so be it, because it is about time to sell this idea. Because I indeed wish it got more takers. Perhaps a metaphor will help: to be an exiled writer is like being a dog or a man hurtled into outer space in a capsule (more like a dog, of course, than a man, because they will never retrieve you). And your capsule is your language. To finish the metaphor off, it must be added that before long the capsule's passenger discovers that it gravitates not earthward but outward.

For one in our profession the condition we call exile is, first of all, a linguistic event: he is thrust, he retreats into his mother tongue. From being his, so to speak, sword, it turns into his shield, into his capsule. What started as a private, intimate affair with the language, in exile becomes fate—even before it becomes an obsession or a duty. A living language, by definition, has a centrifugal propensity—and propulsion; it tries to cover as much ground as possible—and as much emptiness as possible. Hence the population explosion, and hence your autonomous passage outward, into the domain of a telescope or a prayer.

In a manner of speaking, we all work for a dictionary. Because literature *is* a dictionary, a compendium of meanings for this or that human lot, for this or that experience. It is a dictionary of the language in which life speaks to man. Its function is to save the next man, a new arrival, from falling into an old trap, or to help him realize, should he fall into that trap anyway, that he has been hit by a tautology. This way he will be less impressed—and in a way, more free. For to know the meaning of life's terms, of what is happening to you, is liberating. It would seem to me that the condition we call exile is up for a fuller explication; that, famous for its pain, it should also be known for its pain-dulling infinity, for its forgetfulness, detachment, indifference, for its terrifying human and inhuman vistas for which we've got no yardstick except ourselves.

We must make it easier for the next man, if we can't make it safer. And the only way to make it easier for him, to make him less frightened of it, is to give him the whole measure of it—that is, as much as we ourselves can manage to cover. We may argue about our responsibilities and loyalties (toward our respective contemporaries, motherlands, otherlands, cultures, traditions, etc.) ad infinitum, but this responsibility, or rather, opportunity to set the next man—however theoretical he and his needs may be—a bit more free shouldn't become a subject for hesitation. If all this sounds a bit too lofty and humanistic, then I apologize. These distinctions are actually not so much humanistic as deterministic, although one shouldn't bother with such subtleties. All I am trying to say is that, given an opportunity, in the great causal chain of things, we may as well stop being just its rattling effects and try to play causes. The condition we call exile is exactly that kind of opportunity.

Yet if we don't use it, if we decide to remain effects and play exile in an old-fashioned way, that shouldn't be explained away as nostalgia. Of course it has to do with the necessity of telling about oppression, and of course our condition should serve as a warning to any thinking man toying with the idea of an ideal society. That's our value for the free world. That's our function.

But perhaps our greater value and greater function are to be unwitting embodiments of the disheartening idea that a freed man is not a free man, that liberation is just the means of attaining freedom and is not synonymous with it. This highlights the extent of the damage that can be done to the species, and we can feel proud of playing this role. However, if we want to play a bigger role, the role of a free man, then we should be capable of accepting—or at least imitating—the manner in which a free man fails. A free man, when he fails, blames nobody.

Jiří Gruša   I propose that we not discuss this paper. It is very unusual to discuss a paper when the author is not present. We have other papers, by writers who are present, such as Karpinski or Venclova. We can all read Brodsky's paper, but I am opposed to discussing it here.

Nedim Gürsel There is a saying in French to the effect that the absent are always wrong. I find that Brodsky's text raises a number of questions that would give us a better perception of the notion of exile. I myself have a certain number of observations, in particular critical ones, to make in regard to this text.

Richard Kim Mr. Brodsky's paper makes the whole occasion worthwhile to me personally. It is the soul-searching of one writer. I always thought that writers were people who more than anything else examined themselves; I haven't seen much of that so far. When I read Mr. Brodsky's paper, I was ecstatic; it doesn't matter if one agrees with what he says or not. I like the way he presents his ideas. I like the evidence that I find in his paper of one man's desperate search for answers to his own problems. This is someone who has finally learned what it means to be free. And I thought that was the whole point of this gathering. I strongly suggest we discuss the paper. Maybe we will learn something from it.

Nedim Gürsel I find the paper interesting, but there are a number of points that appear obscure to me.

First of all, there is the very notion of exile. I confess to being touched by the reference to the difficult situation of Turkish immigrants in Germany, but what does exile really mean? There seems to be a confusion with regard to the concepts "emigration" and "political exile"; not every exile is a political refugee. In other words, I do not think that the case of a Turkish worker in Germany, interesting as it may be in and of itself, should be identified with that of a political refugee who has been forced to leave his country, or with that of a writer such as Joyce, who lived abroad, or with Hemingway, who spent a great part of his life travelling the world.

My second point is that to Brodsky, the writer in exile seems to be a complete imbecile who does not understand much of anything that is happening around him and who, if he chooses exile, does so because he is fleeing hell. He says, for example, that one flees a bad situation to attain something better. Is this always the case? It is a question I put to myself, and which I put to you as well.

Next he writes that exile is socially insignificant; this is an attitude I find hard to understand. I consider myself a writer in exile, but I am not a political refugee. I do, however, have many compatriots who are political refugees and who live in France. I had difficulties with the government, and was even put on trial, but I did not want to make a career out of that since what interests me above all else is literature. The rest consists of circumstances, which are certainly interesting and important, but which are not the stuff for a writer's career.

I come from a country with a tradition of exile stretching back to the Ottoman Empire, and notably to the time when the "Young Ottomans," as we call them, fled the thirty-three-year absolutist reign of Sultan Akhmed at the end of the nineteenth century. These Young Ottomans were inspired by the ideas of the French Revolution, and it was their struggle which led to the first constitution of 1877 and changed Turkish society. So why present exile only in its negative aspects?

I find that exile can be an enriching experience, one which can lead to greater openness. People come to know other countries, other cultures. And in the process humanity is enriched.

But these are only the negative aspects of Brodsky's text. He reflects notably on the past, to which, he says, the exile's eyes are always turned. He emphasizes the role of memory, saying that it makes itself felt much more sharply in exile than at home. This should encourage us to reflect more carefully about our work, in particular about how we deal in our writing with that memory, which we carry within ourselves.

Edward Limonov   Rather than discuss Brodsky's remarks, I propose that we take up the phenomenon of Brodsky himself. He is an illustration of the star-making process—something that may be all well and good in Hollywood, but which I see as bad for literature. It's not healthy to single out one individual and praise him to the exclusion of everyone else. Is Brodsky the wisest of the exiles? I think not. Is he the best writer?

[Voice from audience: He is!]

It's questionable. He was born to be studied; in my opinion he belongs to the nineteenth century or, rather, to the beginning of the twentieth century. That's why he is so prized; he's so good, he's a dead poet. . . . That's my opinion.

Raissa Orlova   I cannot let those remarks pass. First of all, I think that Brodsky is the greatest . . . [inaudible remark by Limonov]. If one can . . . listen to me, and in any case don't interrupt me. . . . I think Brodsky is a very great poet, and I am glad that he received this great award, given not only to him, but to the grand tradition of Russian poetry and, perhaps, to Russian literature in its present form.

That being said, I must confess that I do not agree fully with everything that Brodsky has written. We have gathered here to talk about the realities of exile, not its possibilities. I share the view (and I have always been of this mind) that emigration is a misfortune. When we left the USSR, my husband and I had return tickets, which we hoped to use in a year or so. Two months later, however, we were stripped of Soviet citizenship. Now, having lived in the West for seven years, I still hold to that same opinion.

Nevertheless, I agree with a statement made here, that emigration is not only a misfortune, but also an opportunity. One aspect of this opportunity, however, was not mentioned either in Brodsky's paper or in any of the speeches which I have heard: by the will of fate, or perhaps contrary to the will of fate, we stand between two worlds and thus have the opportunity to become interpreters between these two worlds—not in the sense of language, or not only in the sense of language, but in the sense of comparing one history with another, of comparing my contemporary reality with another contemporary reality. Today we need to reduce not only the number of rockets, but the hatred, ignorance, and the other abysses that divide people. I believe that this is very important. And it is entirely possible that there is no means more effective for understanding other people than art and poetry.

Antonin Liehm   While agreeing with Raissa Orlova's evaluation of Brodsky, I would also tend to go along with Gruša and Limonov about the so-called "star-making process." That Brodsky is a great writer and poet doesn't give him any special status.

Brodsky says something I believe to be extremely important— that emigration is a new life, not a continuation of the past one. One's sensibility to memories, to the past, naturally becomes terribly important, as do memories of childhood in old age. Old age too is a new life, if you like, but someone who emigrates is entering a world unknown to him. Whatever we may say about writers (and about artists, as well), they always live on the margins, even in their own societies. In this sense it is only a half-truth to say that exile is a new experience. Yet this experience is always unexpected, as Vladimov said, and it is especially difficult after a certain age. For a writer this is even more true, because he is faced not only with a transition of the unconscious, as I said earlier, but with a language transition. In my experience it takes decades to learn to write properly in your own language, so how can you find yet more decades to write properly in a foreign language?

As for Brodsky's assertion that we all feel like complete idiots, this is, I think, an individual perception, and not an absolute rule. The newness, the originality of the experience, may be inevitable, but the sensation of being completely lost is an individual problem; we are more lost in some societies than in others. As a Czech, for example, I probably feel more at home in European society than a Russian writer would, because his experience is so very different. I have also observed that a Czech intellectual feels much more alien, more estranged, from American society than does a Russian writer, because there are similarities between Russian and American societies.

One obvious last item, already mentioned by Limonov: many émigré intellectuals reached a certain degree of social significance which they lost completely on coming out. Brodsky is quite right to bring up the degree of psychological stress this provokes and the need to adapt. Look at the situation of people who are not writers or intellectuals, people whose work is not so urgently linked to individuality, to privacy. They integrate into the new society as immigrants have always done in America. They form groups, begin working together, and set about acquiring a new language. This kind of integration, difficult as it may be, is possible. But how does a writer integrate into a new society? How does he restore his own social role and social significance? It's an enormous strain. The number of suicides among émigré writers and intellectuals has been considerable, and not just in our generation. Look at the German emigration during the Nazi period.

Lastly, I would like to mention our responsibility to the writers in internal exile in the countries which we left. I think we all recognize this responsibility. I agree, however, with what Dovlatov said to Sosnora—that the best people stayed behind and that the crucial questions of a country's literature and culture will not be decided here, but there. We can help, but we cannot resolve such problems.

When Milan Kundera decided not to return to Prague, he wrote a big article for *Le Monde,* in which he attempted to attract the attention of the West to the predicament of the intellectual in Czechoslovakia, and of Czech culture in general. He said that Czechoslovakia had become a cultural desert, that everything was stifled, that everything had died. He had only recently emigrated and he meant well, but the response he got from Czechoslovakia horrified him. The response was one of revulsion; everyone said: "What do you mean? Do you really think that just because you left, everybody else has died?" He learned his lesson and eventually even apologized in a way.

Responsibility thus is a very complex problem, and, while we must do what we can, we must also know our limitations and our proper role.

Libuše Moníková I'm not really comfortable with the idea of returning to Brodsky's comments, any more than I am with his memoirs of Leningrad. Brodsky is first and foremost a poet, and I like some of his poems very much, but his prose is not always so successful. I find that there is too much weeping and wailing both in this paper and in his memoirs. Of course, it's painful to have to leave the country where one grew up, but as an intellectual I find that this sad posturing is simply not an adequate response.

The comparison of an emigrant to a dog shot off into space is typical of Brodsky. These dogs cannot be returned to earth. An intellectual ought to be able to say that he got something positive out of the experience, but you would never know that from Brodsky's writing. When I read things like that, I have a sense of total helplessness.

It really is very difficult to discuss this paper in the absence of the author. I fail to comprehend how he wishes to move on. The examples of the boat people and the *Gastarbeiters* are simply overgeneralized. In spite of all the feelings of loss which we may experience, I am opposed to this sniveling.

Jan Vladislav I am the third Czech in a row to speak. Please forgive us, it's quite by accident.

Reading Brodsky's paper I was reminded of Alma Mahler, wife of the composer. In her autobiography she repeatedly compares emigration to an illness. All well and good, but this illness did not prevent her last husband, Franz Werfel, from writing some important books. In other words, for Alma Mahler, who had to leave a large house, and a society where she was recognized and felt very much at home, emigration was something like a disease. For Franz Werfel, who had already left Czechoslovakia for Austria, and later for France and America, emigration took on an entirely different hue. I think that Alma Mahler confused a social problem with a technical one. I agree with Gürsel—there are times when exile can actually work to the writer's advantage.

When the great Russian poet Alexander Blok was ill with tuberculosis, he went to see his doctor. "Smoking is bad for you," the doctor said. "Living is bad for you," was Blok's reply. In other words, the profession of writing is a dangerous one, perhaps under all regimes. If you write what you think, you are always a danger, even if you live somewhere else.

Jan Novak   I agree with Mr. Vladislav and Mr. Gürsel. Having changed languages, I am an extreme case. I will attempt to explain how that happened and what the implications of this process are for the notion of responsibility.

Mr. Liehm is skeptical about genuinely switching languages, because (as I understand him) in his opinion the unconscious mind is scarcely ever able to negotiate this change. I disagree. I was sixteen when I left Czechoslovakia and seventeen when I arrived in the United States. I didn't speak any English at all, and I started writing poetry—in Czech about Czechs for Czechs. After a time I went to school and began translating my work into English. That is to say, I was still writing in Czech about Czechs, but I was now writing for Americans. Ten years into my stay in the States I noticed that in my dreams even Czechs were speaking English. I think that at that point my unconscious mind was sort of switching gears. I was also getting tired of the tedious and redundant business of translation. So I started to write in English, and I found I was ready for it; work just came pouring out. And my verbal life became more exciting because of this change. At that point I was writing in English, still about Czechs, for Americans. I made the final plunge in my last book, which has no

Czech characters, so now I am writing about Americans in English for Americans.

As for responsibility toward one's native culture, I agree with Mr. Gürsel. The only responsibility I feel is toward literature. It may well be that the fate of the society that I have left will be decided in Czechoslovakia. On the other hand, the fate of Czech literature can be decided anywhere in the world, and even people who, like myself, have switched languages in some sense probably still belong to that literature, and will have some impact on it.

It is now seventeen years since I left, and I have had the eerie experience of reading a Czech translation of a book that I wrote in English. It was my first novel and I had almost written it in Czech, but I wanted to avoid the tedium of translating a long book, so in the end I decided to write it in English.

A year ago a translation of the work was produced in Prague, and was done very well. I sat down and read it, and it was my book, my characters, my story, my words, the same rhythms and long breathless sentences. But I could never have written that book. Had I written it in Czech, it would have been a totally different book, so I was sitting there, with this strange mirror, looking at myself as I had been seventeen years ago. I saw how arrested my linguistic development in Czech was and how American the voice was, and it was a very powerful and odd experience.

Yury Miloslavsky　Returning to Brodsky, I would like to say that everyone is well aware how foolish it would be to deny that writers in the confines of a particular literature and time frame are competitors. This being the case, I think we should attempt to maintain a polite and intelligent objectivity and not lapse into name-calling. Not only that, we should try to speak of each other elegantly. It matters for literature in general, but especially to Russian literature. I regret that, for some reason, my friend and colleague Edward Limonov, whom I have known for a number of years, did not show sufficient restraint when talking about Joseph Brodsky and called him a dead poet. We may be witnessing a psychological incompatibility here. I think Joseph Brodsky is a great Russian poet, and I hope he lives "through the ages."

Brodsky, it seems to me, has been extraordinarily lucky. He

really is a great poet who is recognized by his contemporaries and loved by them. More than that, he is understood, loved and published by people who have no understanding of literature, and that is a real miracle—a miracle without parallel, at least in my knowledge. Someone said that Brodsky is "just one of us." That is not quite true, because Brodsky is a great Russian poet. Since there is no other great Russian poet in this hall, I believe that we should reconcile ourselves to this accomplished fact.

Anton Shammas   Russians! May I have your attention please! I am going to attack you. Put your headphones on, and sharpen your weapons.

Today I feel like a caterpillar trapped in somebody else's cocoon. In this instance it's an Eastern European cocoon. Where I come from we have a lot of Russians, and Yury [Miloslavsky] is one of them. There are a lot of Russians talking about Russian problems and Russians in exile. Everywhere I go, I seem to be driven away by Russians.

Perhaps I am being paranoid, but this feeling was heightened by the opening sentence of Brodsky's paper (which I happen to like). "As we gather here, in this attractive and well-lit room on this cold December evening," he said, "to discuss the plight of the writer in exile, let us pause for a minute and think of those who quite naturally didn't make it to this room." This sentence gives me the ultimate sense of exile. Here I am in a room, which is being described for me by somebody else. I have problems of my own with this room, and along comes Brodsky describing the room, without even being here, to me, a person driven out of Israel by Russians. [Laughter, applause.]

I was trying to promote an idea that haunts me, and that has to do with direction. I am bilingual and write in Arabic and Hebrew; both languages are written from right to left. I assume that all the people here, except perhaps Nuruddin, who comes from an oral culture, write from left to right.

The Swiss art historian Heinrich Woelfflin wrote an article about left and right in art, in which he discussed eighteenth-century landscape painting, the Flemish school and European art in general. He began by describing a situation similar to one we might experience today. Imagine we are watching slides of Raphael's Sistine Madonna projected onto a screen. On the left is Pope Sixtus, looking up at the Madonna holding the Child. Her mantle flows down toward St. Barbara, on the right of the picture. St. Barbara is pointing toward two bambinos, who are at the bottom of the picture looking upward.

Now imagine the slide in reverse: St. Barbara is looking down at the two bambinos; you are lost—you miss the whole point, you don't see the subject of the picture, the Madonna. You expect the landscape to be viewed from left to right, as is the case with ninety-nine percent of European paintings. Just as you write from left to right, you expect the subject of the sentence to start from the left and end at the right. So in landscapes, there is usually a sort of path going through the picture, and you follow that path in order to understand the picture.

I am now sitting in a room described by Mr. Brodsky as well lit. It's not well lit at all. It's badly lit. And I'm trying to explain to myself why I am not understanding anything that the Russian writers are saying. And not only the Russians, but the other Eastern Europeans as well. It is as if I were seeing the slide in reverse; I understood every word, and I followed the translation very meticulously, but the words don't make sense to me. Am I missing something?

Richard Kim   I was thinking about what exile used to be like. When I left my country I came on a slow boat from China, and it took three weeks to get to America. But nowadays we're in the jet age, when people are physically transported from one society to another in a few hours. Moreover, we now live in an age of mass media, mass communication, and instant information.

Another point of difference between then and now is that we're seeing a lot more generosity than in the old days. I seem to sense that a lot of you are doing very well, compared to what I had to go through.

As for the Brodsky paper, I found a number of things in it perplexing, but I was truly impressed by his last sentence: "A free man, when he fails, blames nobody." When I read that line I knew exactly, I thought, what he had to go through, how much intellect and emotion had gone into that one line. This is what it means to be free, to accept the tremendous, awesome, terrifying responsibilities of freedom and its consequences.

Nedim Gürsel   I would like to reassure Shammas that he is not alone in being paranoid. I have experienced some of that same feeling in listening to the comments of my Russian colleagues. I find their experiences very interesting, but they have no relevance to my own experience as a writer in exile.

Take, for example, Brodsky's comment about the loss of social status. That is typical of an exile from the East. What social status?

In Turkey the writer has no social status. I will give you an example from my own experience. I wrote a novel which is called *La première femme* and which describes the first sexual experiences of an adolescent in certain areas in Istanbul which are not actually red light districts, but where he gets to know the female body, and along with it the life of the city. The book was confiscated for offending public morality, and I found myself before a judge, who said to me: "Do you not feel guilty? You are a professor at the Sorbonne (suddenly I had a certain social status in his eyes) and you allow yourself to write books which make us blush with shame!" At first he used the familiar form of address with me, since—as a writer—I had no social status. In view of my status as a teacher, however, he advised me to cease and desist, and acquitted me (by the way, very kindly).

We spoke of Socrates at the beginning of this conference. Perhaps we should also have spoken of Plato, who banished poets from his Republic, and I also think of a *Surah* from the Koran, which is otherwise called the *Surah* of the poets, which says that one must not follow poets because they have strayed from the true path, so for me to be a writer, by definition, means for me that I have no social status at all.

Nuruddin Farah I would like to ask a question of my Russian, Czech and Polish friends, since their condition of exile differs absolutely from mine. I come from Somalia, which is ruled by a dictator, and the day this dictator is overthrown is the very day that I will book my flight back to Somalia. Whether I will survive the dictatorship that will take over, once this dictatorship is overthrown, is another question, and one I don't want to ask myself. Forgive me if I am naive, but I would like my Eastern European friends to imagine the unimaginable: if the opportunity were to arise for them to return—for good— would they do so?

Edward Limonov I will never go back. Everyone chooses his place of residence, and I am not such an idiot as to leave Paris for Moscow. I have even acquired French citizenship.

Having said that, I must also say that my attitude has no connection to politics. If you would read my books you would understand who I am and that I have nothing to do with Russians at all. I am the writer uprooted; true, I operate with the Russian language, but my first three books deal with American reality. Only now, when I have to give something to my publishers to make money, do I write about Russia. Not only will I never return, I don't even want to make a short visit; it doesn't interest me. I don't want to return to my past. I would rather go to Africa, and see the new reality. If they want to publish me over there, that's fine. It's a big market in the Soviet Union—265 million people.

Raissa Orlova   The complaint has been made that Russian topics have been monopolizing our discussion. At the risk of raising the level of Russian and general-European paranoia, I must say that those who spoke before me should have recognized that the events in my native land (which is, after all, a superpower) will determine not only our existence—that of my friends and relatives—but also your existence. Unfortunately, Russian events are not a local problem. For that reason, I do not believe that we are dealing with a narrow, provincial, local paranoia, but with a far more widespread phenomenon.

Someone here made a statement I would like to discuss. It does not matter who the speaker was, since I have often heard that comment before. I refer to the claim that everything that has happened in the Soviet Union over the last two years is merely for show, to fool the West, that it is window dressing irrelevant to the true development of literature—our current topic of discussion. I believe that this view is totally out of step with reality, and people making such statements are either blind, or do not wish to see. I am not speaking about official speeches, or about Gorbachev, but about what is happening in literature. It is true that we have no great works as of yet, but neither do I find them in places where censorship does not exist. We are witnessing an enormous effort on the part of many, many people to reevaluate their past and present. We can see this written in black and white, published in large press runs in the Soviet Union.

When I and some of my comrades who are here today lived there, we got involved with what is referred to in the Penal Code as "possession and distribution." We retyped, translated, and distributed to each other works such as the poems of Anna Akhmatova, Marina Tsvetaeva, Boris Pasternak, and Boris Slutsky, Solzhenitsyn's short stories and novels, Vladimov's novel *Faithful Ruslan*, and Voinovich's novel *The Life and Extraordinary Adventures of Private Ivan Chonkin*. During the last year we in the free world have spent our time photocopying Soviet magazines—novels, articles, verse. The mail carries our packages back and forth, because not all of us subscribe to the Soviet magazines *Znamya, Ogonyok, Moskovskie novosti,* etc. At the same time, this is vitally important to us. The very fact that not only I, but many others as well, are doing this is proof of what is happening. Many new areas are no longer taboo for discussion. No one could even hint at these topics before, but now they are brought up in Soviet magazines.

Now that our amazement has passed, we must begin to think through what is happening and attempt to comprehend how this will effect our lives. Someone joked that *perestroika* (restructuring) is taking place only in the area of *nadstroika* (the Marxist concept of "superstructure"). Thus it is not "being" which "determines consciousness," but the reverse. Articles have appeared in Moscow such as Burtin's "For a Different Generation," published in *October,* or Karyakin's "Should We Step on the Rake?" in *Znamya.* These deserve *very* serious consideration, and it is, I believe, an important task that should be undertaken by émigré writers. *Glasnost* has taken on such phenomenal proportions that, a mere year ago, we could not even have conceived of such changes.

Why is everyone in such a hurry? Why do people on both sides of the border keep asking if there is anything new? Is there anything in the latest issue of this or that journal? Perhaps it will all be gone by tomorrow? What will happen tomorrow? All of us—both here and there—are swept up by this common mood. Something that is being discussed in the Soviet press, but that has not yet materialized, is the creation of a mechanism which would make all this irrevocable. Why? Because there is nothing in the mechanism of state, in the law code, that can guarantee that the old ways will not return.

My husband and I correspond with a number of people in Moscow, and just before coming here we received a letter. A friend of ours had visited a club named "Perestroika." As is the case with the majority of such informal organizations, this club has no constitution or program. It recognizes only three "no's": no violence, no chauvinism, and no monopoly on absolute truth. The monopolistic possession of absolute truth is one of the major diseases of the Russian émigré community. Perhaps other émigré groups suffer from this affliction as well; I am not well-enough informed to judge.

If each of us does his best to cure himself of this disease and attempts to hear the voices of the rest of the world, we will all have a better chance to understand each other and solve our problems. We need to see the world from a different angle, from the other side.

I don't know how the rest of you feel, but I am torn between hope and despair. Sometimes it seems to me that we are a "lonely crowd" where no one understands anyone else. Everybody talks at once, and their voices pass the others by unheard. But at other times it seems to me that we have here a piece of the world republic of the spirit which could serve as the foundation of that society which we wish for our children and grandchildren.

To quote Limonov, I am one of those "idiots" who not only want to visit Moscow, but even dream of it. Since Brezhnev's death, I have submitted five visa applications . . . and received five refusals. But I still hope to see the day it will happen.

People here have said we should avoid creating a cult of personality around Brodsky. I agree with that, and for that reason I wish to close my remarks with the words of another poet, one living in Russia, David Samoilov:

> Where can I flee from my native land,
> From its eternal mirages
> Reaching out like bushes in my path?
> Where can I flee from the Russian word,
> So young, so naked,
> From the song of tragedy . . .

Anton Shammas Earlier on, when addressing my Russian friends, it seems I was not sufficiently blunt. They do not seem to have understood me—just as I often fail to grasp their points. Since we are running out of both patience and Russians, I want to make one brief remark, to deliver a coup de grâce, in case they feel neglected.

Please correct me if I am wrong, but the Russians seem to think they have a monopoly on exile. They seem to think that their situation is the most important thing in the world.

I come from a place which V. S. Naipaul once described as the half-made societies of the Third World, and I think that today that world, not Russia, is the primary issue. I know Russia runs the world, but I ask you not to ignore our problems.

I appreciate Brodsky and I am pleased that he received the Nobel Prize, but I am afraid that this act will concentrate world attention on Russian literature for another ten or twenty years. Frankly, I am sick and tired of Russian literature. [Applause]

Nuruddin Farah   Earlier I said we were all driven from Paradise when Adam and Eve were expelled from Heaven. My idea of home presupposes the nostalgic return. If, as in the case of Limonov and some of the others, there is no notion of return, what do we use to replace that sense of nostalgia?

Anton Shammas   Nuruddin, the Garden of Eden is a masterpiece of boredom; who wants to go there? Exile is far more interesting. I would support expulsion from the Garden of Eden, because it makes life and literature more interesting. You go home only through your own language; otherwise the road is blocked.

Antonin Liehm   We really cannot pose general questions such as "Do the Russians (or the Czechs) want to return or not?" The answers will inevitably differ from individual to individual.

With regard to Mr. Shammas's argument, I agree that the main reason the West cares for Russian refugees is that it sees them as part of the East-West struggle. It is true that they are more welcome than refugees from Africa, Israel, or elsewhere, but they are not to be blamed for that.

Nedim Gürsel   It is true that the East-West conflict exists and that it is a real conflict, but we must not forget that the earth is round. I recently participated in Paris in a gathering of European writers, where we discussed, among other things, the difficulties Turkey has been encountering for over a century now in becoming a European country. It was basically a gathering of European writers and, being a Turkish writer, I felt a bit uneasy. Still, I feel that geography does not mean a great deal, because the closer one moves toward the West, the more likely he is to find himself in the East.

I perceive this gathering as one dominated by Russian ethnocentrism. You could argue that this orientation is justifiable on the grounds that Russia, or the Soviet Union, is a great country, and that Russian literature is important. Nevertheless, a gathering whose theme is the writer in exile should not, in my opinion, limit itself to Russian writers.

I happen to have just written a book about the Turkish poet Nâzim Hikmet, who was a great innovator in poetry. I recommend to you his book *Exile Is a Hard Trade*. He chose liberty and died in exile—in Moscow, after having spent fifteen years in Turkish prisons. Personally, I would have chosen a different place of exile from Moscow. I might mention in passing that I like living in Paris.

In the film *Voyage à Cythère* by the Greek producer Angelopoulous, the central character is an exiled Greek who has spent much of his life in the countries of the East. This character interests me because he was an exile many times over. He was an Anatolian; that is, a Greek from Anatolia who underwent the dire consequences of what the Greeks call the "Great Catastrophe"; in other words, the expulsion of the Greek population from Anatolia after the Turkish War of Independence. An exile in a country which he felt to be his own (Greece), he was actually an Anatolian. After the Greek Civil War he was exiled to the place where most of my Russian colleagues come from.

I mention these two writers to illustrate to my Russian friends that the earth is round, and that the place of exile can vary not only on the basis of political opinions, but also from individual to individual.

I may have exaggerated the degree of Russian ethnocentrism here, and it may even be completely justified in a gathering like ours, but at the same time we must not forget that there have been others.

Lev Kopelev I thank my Turkish colleague for having mentioned Nâzim's name; it's high time that we did that. Nâzim Hikmet was our friend. We loved him in life, and we accompanied him to the grave. His exile experience can teach us a good deal. Nâzim came almost straight from a Turkish jail to Russia in the difficult period 1950–51. He had not seen Russia for almost thirty years, and he arrived with the idealized concepts he took away with him at the age of twenty, when he witnessed the tumult of the revolution and, with Mayakovsky, spoke before large audiences. His was a bitter disappointment—so bitter that he even suffered a heart attack. But how he worked together with his Russian colleagues and friends during the "Thaw"—and not just with friends!

I first saw Nâzim while I myself was in prison, a much better prison than we had been in formerly. After Stalin's death, we even had a television. I saw Nâzim speak out against dogmatism in art, in his wonderful, broken Russian, which, though heavily accented, was fully comprehensible. This to me was a spectacle of great spiritual courage.

At that time we all had our illusions. He believed in a socialist revolution that would make all men happy. He believed that the things he experienced in Russia were a distortion, a false path. We quarreled heatedly. He defended his views with passion, but he was far more devoted to Turkey than any one of us was to Russia.

We were not the only ones he helped. There are Polish friends here. Perhaps they know what it meant when Nâzim accepted Polish citizenship on visiting Warsaw in 1955. He talked to the people about the first "Warsaw Thaw" and about the trips he made in the last years of his life.

Nâzim is an example of someone who made his life productive both as a writer and a human being. I thank you for having mentioned him. I'm sorry I did not think to do so myself.

Adam Zagajewski   I am from Poland. I live in a Parisian suburb. I write poetry and essays. I don't want to take sides here, not the Russian side, nor even the side of Poland.

We are having difficulty defining the intellectual paradigm of our time. Our colleagues from the Third World seem not to understand that the struggle between East and West is also, or mainly, a struggle between the totalitarian mind and the nontotalitarian mind. Since many Third World countries are very much involved in this struggle, I don't think it irrelevant to discuss certain totalitarian problems.

I tried to make a great statement about exile. I didn't succeed, it's so overwhelming a subject. Exile is like birth. There are so many disadvantages, and some joys, both in being born and being in exile.

I'd like first to address Mr. Limonov, who presented the Soviet Union as a defenseless country. His simple-minded remarks need a simple-minded reply. I would like to remind him that this conference would not be necessary if the Soviet army didn't occupy half of Europe.

You can hardly help noticing that the atmosphere among us exiled writers is not the best. We seem full of bitterness and resentment. Even the brilliant text prepared by Joseph Brodsky is not actually benign. I don't think that what we are observing here is merely the dictates of a universal law that decrees that exiles quarrel more than people who didn't leave their country. I think something more important is happening. The postwar generation of Eastern European exiles perceived as its role the clear-cut but extremely difficult task of denouncing Communist totalitarianism. In the late forties and early fifties Western attitudes toward them were generally hostile, and this hostility only made them more obstinate in defending their views. Theirs was the side of reason and democracy. They wanted to oppose totalitarianism—in a creative way.

Today's exiles, many of whom I know, on the whole enjoy better conditions, but the grand task of denouncing the inhuman nature of totalitarianism has already, in some sense, been accomplished. Totalitarianism didn't disappear, alas, but intellectually it has not become more attractive. Antonin Liehm said that we are fed up with anti-Communist conferences. I, for one, am not, if only because I do not participate in them.

I believe that our generation of exiles must now attempt to redefine our spiritual destiny, our spiritual work. The brilliant books on totalitarianism have been already written—by Orwell, Koestler, Miłosz, and many others. What can we do? Our tragedy is that totalitarianism was not destroyed, because human thought, human ideas do not destroy anything.

It may be boring to go on and on again about Soviet tanks and censorship, but such things do exist.

In Polish intellectual life, as in my own intellectual life, there is a significant ambivalence about the relationship between politics and art. In the Polish, Czech, and Russian clandestine press, there are voices saying: "Be political, be critical, be rational." But there are other voices saying: "Be artistic, be metaphysical." I hear the same voices inside my own head. It may be that the struggle of these two voices is an ancient one, but I think this dualism is particularly significant for our time, and perhaps for my generation.

Our notion of reality is very imperfect, fragmented and contradictory. Reality was never as impenetrable as it is now. Totalitarianism has become boring; we know too much about it. But what should we do about it?

A friend of mine wrote once the following line: "The greatest Polish poet is the state." Totalitarian states are in fact poets, false poets; they try to impose their meaning on the world. There is, or should be, war between poetry and totalitarianism. Writing is the search for meaning, for the magic transformation of reality into poetry. Totalitarianism doesn't look for meaning, it has already found it. This rivalry cannot be made milder by any compromise.

The French philosopher Simone Weil once drew a distinction between *la pesanteur* and *la grâce*—gravity and grace. Gravity stands for the cruel determinism of the physical and even the human world, while grace stands for rare episodes of nobility. Writing is like grace: it comes, it disappears, it is sympathetic magic, it lends meaning to reality. This disjunction between gravity and writing is perhaps even stronger in exile. In some happy countries, that we perhaps imagine as having existed only in fiction or in the past, poetry and architecture were not torn apart as strongly as they are now. To write in exile means to be cut off from civilization. It's only art, it's only inspiration, it's only a poem, people say. It's not architecture, it's not civilization. The increased tension between gravity and grace in exile is not necessarily a disaster. A nineteenth-century philosopher said: *Ubi pater sum, ibi patria*: "Where I create (where I become father), there is my fatherland."

Edward Limonov It's true that I belonged to a totalitarian state, but I exchanged my status for that of the Third World. Please, put me in the Third World.

In 1602 there was a Polish king in Moscow. Now things have changed. History has always been unjust. But you cannot refight history by fighting Russian writers. You have to fight history with brute force and tanks. Like it or not, the current situation in Europe was set up by the Russian army. Change it, fight them, kill them, then talk. That is all I wanted to say.

Lev Kopelev   They are not Russian troops, but Soviet troops! There is a big difference!

Edward Limonov   That has nothing to do with reality.

Lev Kopelev   That is absolute reality!

Anton Shammas   I want to stir the embers once again. [Laughter in the audience.] I love to watch East European minds at work. . . .
      I think you are all in big, big trouble if you think that poetry can fight totalitarianism. Mr. Brodsky claims: "We must somehow maintain that literature is the only form of moral insurance that a society has." Come on! Let's face it. Society does not have any moral insurance.

Adam Zagajewski   I'd like to answer Anton Shammas.
      I do not write political poems and I do not believe that poetry can fight totalitarianism. As both a rational and an irrational being, I think my poems are written by my irrational self. Still, I think that poetry, the neighborhood of poetry, carries with it a vision of the world. I am not a moralist poet and I'm not a political poet, so I expect I have been misunderstood. I simply put forward certain misgivings that I harbor about the nature of the world, as well as a vision of the world which may be mine or may be that of my generation. In the Polish cultural scene, I'm against political poetry and so-called poetry *engagé*. You missed the point.

Anton Shammas   I was asking you if you really believe that poetry can fight the state. If you don't, our positions do not differ.

Lev Kopelev   Not fight the state, but defend human beings, the human soul!

Libuše Moníková   I wish to raise a linguistic objection. As writers we should be quite precise in our use of terms. We are not dealing here solely with the Third World. We always begin with the Third World, or with the fourth. Seldom are the first or second worlds discussed.

As writers, we should, in general, avoid these concepts. The same is true of the comfortable but incorrect concepts "East" and "West." What is our point of orientation in using such concepts? If you look at a map of Europe, you will see that Prague and Czechoslovakia are clearly in the west. The "middle" begins somewhere around Minsk. Kundera, for example, vehemently rejects the concept of "Eastern Europe" and speaks of "Central Europe." Europe ends at the Urals. According to this definition Moscow is also a Western city, and from our vantage point here in Vienna, Prague is clearly Western. What are "East" and "West," and what is the "Third World?"

Jan Vladislav   It has been asked whether poetry can be dangerous to a regime. Since regimes put poets in prison, the answer is, evidently, yes.

Adam Zagajewski   A word or two for Anton Shammas: yes, I think that poetry can fight the state. I don't think it can win this war, though there were brilliant poets, like Mandelstam, or like Vladimír Holan, who tried.

The shadow of the state is present in poetry, but the fight is, nevertheless, hopeless.

Richard Kim   I keep going back to the main theme of this conference—the importance of the exiled writer. Just what sort of image do we have of ourselves and how do we define ourselves? Someone here has said that the whole concept of exile is a holdover from nationalism and nation-states and so forth, and that some day, when nation-states and nationalism disappear, the term "exile" will cease to exist. A wonderful concept; I was very much taken by it.

I sense that some of us are trying to define ourselves as writers in exile. On an individual plane, that's a very lonesome job. On the other hand, some of us seem to be working toward a collective sense of identification. I can't quite put my finger on it, and I'm not saying that everyone in that group is consciously thinking or saying: I'm a member of this group, therefore I should do this or that, but there seems to be some sort of abstract collective sense present here. I feel very lonely when I face people who think like that, because I'm obsessively interested in my own small, private problem, as an exile, as a writer. Still, I must confess to envying them; at the very least, I wish them luck.

In having been suddenly transplanted into a different cultural setting, where only the individual is valued, I learned a bitter lesson: it didn't matter what I was back home. Americans simply said: "Oh yeah? Prove it. Show it to me." I had to start life all over again, from scratch. The writer's profession is a very, very private business.

Wojciech Karpinski

The Exile as Writer: A
Conversation about
Sorrow and Joy

What is it like to be a writ-
er in exile? What are the writer's ties with the community he has
left? With his new surroundings? A great deal depends, of course, on
what we mean by the expression "writer in exile." We could dwell on
the merits of various definitions, or we could compile personal statements. I shall take a third road. The topic is a painful one. It is hard to
be objective about it. A subjective tone is equally constraining. Perhaps we can contrive to say more by listening to what others have had
to say—in moments of honesty.

It so happens that for two centuries emigration has been the
destiny of Polish literature. In other countries *some* works have
arisen in exile. The *fundamental* works of Polish literature, those
which shaped its language and imagination, arose outside the borders
of the country. This is what happened in the nineteenth century:
after the defeat of 1831 there was a *sudden* explosion of creativity. In
the space of just a few months there arose in Dresden, and above all in
Paris, innovative works, quickly recognized by the émigrés and then
by the entire country as an expression of Polish society's aspirations.
In the twentieth century, after the defeats of 1939 and 1945, the
situation developed differently. Today we understand that the postwar Polish émigré community, particularly in the persons of Witold
Gombrowicz and Czesław Miłosz, created a great literature. Their
contemporaries, both in Poland and in exile, had a different opinion.

The writers themselves had a different opinion. They felt they were a minority within a minority, doubly exiled—from their homeland and from émigré society. If one can speak of a no-win situation in a writer's exile experience, then it certainly would apply to their cases. When Czesław Miłosz decided to stay in the West in 1951, he began his first work in emigration (and directed to the émigré community) with the words, "What I am about to describe can be called the story of a certain suicide." From today's perspective his words appear astonishing and self-evidently unjust, in relation both to himself and to émigré society. But perhaps it was owing to this attitude that he was able to discern and to help others discern the sorrows and joys of exile.

One can construct out of the works of Gombrowicz and Miłosz a conversation about the situation of the writer in exile. This conversation had a fundamental significance for them. They had to discover who they were, what their ties were with society and with tradition, what threatened and what challenged them. They had to direct their gaze at themselves, achieve freedom by naming limitations. Now they have become an example of freedom for others.

The conversation about the sorrows and joys of exile which was conducted by postwar Polish émigrés can be broken down into voices. As the starting point of this conversation I take an essay by Emil Cioran, a Rumanian who writes in excellent French. It was published in the Paris-based journal *Kultura* in June 1952, in Witold Gombrowicz's translation and with his commentary. Cioran's essay appeared in his book, *La tentation d'exister* (The Temptation to Exist) and was called "Avantages de l'exil" in French; in Polish it bears the title, "Dogodnośći i niedogodnośći wygnania," or "The Advantages and Disadvantages of Exile."

Cioran is provocative. He deliberately draws a portrait that is a caricature. He is not afraid of judging unjustly and therefore hits the mark forcefully more than once. And sometimes through his one-sidedness he reveals errors of extreme and hasty judgment. For him, the writer in exile is a competitive and embittered individual. The exile yearns to bring his name to the attention of others at any price. How can he do this? After all, he writes in an unknown language. Translation? He won't find a translator. And if he does find one, the translation will be a travesty. And who will publish it? Who will put out a hand to select his exotic book? Should he write in another language? How many people can manage that? And if he does manage it, he becomes someone else, he performs a heroic betrayal, breaks with the past and, to a certain extent, with himself.

What should he write about and how? He yearns to tell other people about his misfortune. His subject matter is soon exhausted. One can't keep on repeating the image of exile, and that is why, in Cioran's opinion, the novel is not a genre for the exile. His element is poetry. Prose demands a differentiated social base, traditions, precision. Poetry gushes; it is direct and also completely fanciful; it is the domain of troglodytes and aesthetes. In the beginning, the ground slips out from under the feet of exiles. For a poet, that is a privileged position. Think how much effort it cost Rilke to lose one fatherland after another, to break his ties with the world. The exile achieves this condition at a cheap price. But the threat is that he will become accustomed to exile, that he will be an epigone of his own despair. The source of his inspiration will dry up. Depending on his temperament, he will seek salvation by indulging in piety or in sarcasm. Faith or humor—those are the final stations of the writer in exile, as Cioran envisions him.

Gombrowicz responded to these lightning-quick simplifications in his "Commentary," which he later expanded in his *Diary*. Cioran's words reek of the mustiness of the grave, but they are too pusillanimous. Who is this "writer in exile"? Mickiewicz wrote books and Mr. X writes perfectly proper, even readable, books; both are "writers" and, *nota bene*, writers in exile. And with that the similarity between them ends. There are various kinds of exile: Rimbaud, Norwid, Kafka. . . . Every great writer, as a consequence of his greatness, was a foreigner in his own land. Many of them wrote against their readers, not for them. They became famous because they valued themselves more than success. Every work of art, Gombrowicz adds, not just émigré art, arises in the closest contact with disintegration and is health created out of illness. Every work of art brushes up against absurdity. Art in general is a cemetery of ambitions; for every work that manages to come to fruition there are thousands that remain unfulfilled. A lack of honors, of support of one's native community? But such a hothouse atmosphere encourages artificial hierarchies. The writer whom Cioran describes never really existed, in Gombrowicz's opinion; he is just the embryo of a writer.

The immersion in the world that is exile should, in theory, create an opportunity for literature. The elite of the country are expelled beyond its borders. They can think, feel and write from the outside. They achieve distance. They achieve spiritual freedom. Writers ought to speak in a strong, independent voice. But that's not what happens, Gombrowicz comments. Why? Because they are too free. Lost in the world, they are afraid; they cling convulsively to the past, they cling to each other. They are afraid of their own freedom. They cling to a single hope—that of regaining their fatherland. It seems to them that the collective strength of émigré society can arise only from renouncement of the ego. Along with other blindness, the writer tries to inflict on himself and his countrymen a blind faith. Disinterested thought becomes a dangerous luxury. Such a writer is unable to exist without his fatherland. On the altar of this ideal fatherland he disavows intellectual independence; he ceases to be a writer.

The threat to the writer in exile is the view of emigration as a collectivity that pretends to authority over souls and that takes away the writer's freedom. The two greatest Polish writers of the twentieth century, Gombrowicz and Miłosz, did not struggle solely or primarily with an external threat, with the imposed Communist ideology; they also struggled with internal threats, with the marasmus of emigration as an institution, with their own blindness. In these difficult and painful battles, each of them sought support within himself and came to learn the truth about himself.

Gombrowicz warned Miłosz that he should not yield to the "tyranny of the straw men of abstraction," that he should not allow himself to be blackmailed by "historical necessities" and "social demands and obligations," that he should not demonize exile and loneliness. Gombrowicz tried to be spiritually free, open to reality and loyal to it. He decided to speak only about what he really knew: about his own reality. Charges of egotism pursued him for many years. Only in time did people come to understand that this posture was a kind of liberating asceticism. His judgment of the émigré community was severe and similar to his judgment of literature back in Poland: a stagnant puddle. His policy was to look the situation in the eye. To be alive, in all senses: "not to be a statue; not to be a professional mourner; not to be a grave digger; not to recite; not to repeat oneself; not to exaggerate; not to belittle; not to thunder and roar; not to indulge in witticisms. And above all—re-evaluate! Re-evaluate everything we possess, and in addition, re-evaluate ourselves." Gombrowicz realized his goal despite the émigré community, by irritating it, provoking it to react. He said to himself, "I majored in freedom, and the school of exile intensified what was in me from birth: the bitter joy of taking leave of that which takes leave of me." In this "school of exile" Gombrowicz studied himself first of all. He spoke about himself and that is why he was heard, though belatedly; his work was a lesson in individual freedom. Like Nietzsche, he teaches us how to lose what can be lost—and how, in exile, to find oneself, to transform loss into gain. This is not a magic formula, but a continually renewed effort.

Their rebellion against the official émigré hierarchies was a common factor linking Miłosz with Gombrowicz. The forms and sources of their rebellion were different, however. Miłosz at first saw exile as death for a poet. Later he viewed his situation more calmly. Rebellious impulses kept returning: rebellion against the society he had left, against the society that surrounded him, against the émigré community, against the West, against himself. He defines himself, in moments of depression, as a man who does not accept this earth and this heaven, who is seeking, always in vain, for a different heaven, a different earth. At other times, in moments of joy, he manages to describe with unequaled precision and expressiveness his delight in the particular moment, in the place where he happens to be, whether Lithuania or Mazowsze, the streets of Paris or the valley of the Dordogne, the Sierra Nevada or San Francisco Bay.

Miłosz once remarked that his first emigration occurred when he moved to Warsaw from Vilno before the war. In *The Land of Ulro* he reaches even deeper into the past; he describes his exile from the paradise of childhood. In his work one can follow the concentric circles of exile that present themselves to him with differing degrees of intensity in different periods of his life. In 1967 he noted:

Exile is the fate of the contemporary poet, regardless of whether he lives in his native land or abroad, because he is almost always torn away from the little familiar world of customs and beliefs that he knew in his childhood. In and of itself exile is neither good nor bad; romantic and pathetic gestures are useless in this situation, and can only lead to falsehood. Exile simply has to be accepted and everything depends on what use is made of it. In any event, one must discard the myth of creative impotence that supposedly afflicts the poet from the moment the mystic bond that connects him with his native land is severed. Such a view bears the stamp of the peasant civilizations that, for better or worse, are beginning to belong to the past.

Miłosz's admission does not mean that he had attained an Olympian equanimity. The bitter aspects of emigration had not vanished. Instead of writing in Polish, he complains he might as well place his manuscripts in hollow trees, for all the success they have. What about writing in another language? His relations with foreigners are too superficial. Poles he finds far too irritating. It is easy to touch a raw nerve; they are a part of him, Miłosz, his *le moi haïssable.* That is why, he confessed elsewhere (in *The Land of Ulro*), his writing for foreigners was only a pragmatic or didactic effort, since he doesn't believe deeper understanding is possible outside a shared language and shared historical tradition.

In his essay "Notes on Exile," Miłosz demonstrated in a more complicated fashion the joys and limitations of writing. This text, published in 1975, can be read as a continuation of the conversation with Gombrowicz. There are also evident analogies with Cioran's text, although Miłosz attempts to discern more nuances. Miłosz believes that exile, accepted as destiny, can help expose our delusions. At present, the censorship in totalitarian countries permits various little avant-garde games that were once forbidden. It strikes mercilessly, however, when the writer shows an interest in his surrounding reality. If that same writer should find himself in exile, either by choice or because he has been banished, he will consider it his duty to keep on spouting his personal observations. However, what was treated with deadly seriousness in his own country is of concern to very few people abroad, even if, for accidental reasons, it happens to arouse some interest. Thus the writer concludes that he cannot address those who are interested in his subject matter; he can only address those with whom he has no direct understanding. Gradually he is sucked into the life of the country to which he has emigrated, and his knowledge of the country from which he comes changes from the tangible to the theoretical. If he remains interested in the same problems as before, his work will lose its immediacy. Thus, if he does not want to be condemned to sterility, he must undergo a deep transformation.

The writer in exile needs *new eyes*, says Miłosz. Whether he will have the strength to cover this new distance depends on resources, of which the exile has very little prior knowledge. He can try to change his language. He can do this literally, writing in the language of his adopted country, or he can use his native tongue in such a way that what he writes will be understood and accepted by his new public. In that case, however, he ceases, in Miłosz's opinion, to be an exile. A more difficult path lies in his preserving a theoretical, imaginary presence in his country of origin. An imaginary presence—because the writer must conceive of his country's literature as an organism that is developing over time and must assign to his own work a function in this movement from past to present. That is Miłosz's fundamental thesis. He is very close to Gombrowicz on this point. Both of them were continually searching for the living roots of their native culture by settling accounts with its past. They observed the present critically. They kept their distance from the literary community of both their homeland and the émigré community. For they felt that they were *the future of their native literature*. That was their true community; they wished to occupy a prominent position in it. That is why they criticized so passionately what they considered to be the false hierarchies of the past and the present. One can find in the works of both these writers demystifying histories of Polish literature, particularly of contemporary literature, and also a merciless analysis of contemporary Western culture.

Miłosz argues that certain styles and literary genres, such as the realistic novel, by their very nature cannot be maintained in exile. On the other hand, exile, which forces one to look closely at the world from different perspectives, favors other genres and styles, particularly those which deal in the symbolic transformation of reality. According to Miłosz, three main causes for despair are particularly potent in the first stage of exile: the loss of one's name, the fear of failure, and moral anguish.

The loss of one's name: the writer shapes his image in large measure by discerning it in the eyes of those who react to his works.

When he emigrates, the image becomes blurred and the writer himself becomes an anonymous component of the masses.

The fear of failure: he belonged to a community of writers who dedicated themselves to a certain ritual in which they dispensed praise and scorn to each other; he has lost his point of reference, and he begins to think that he never was able to stand on his own legs.

The understanding of failure, that is, of the wavering of the collective point of reference, is a condition for achieving victory. But this victory is morally suspect. The writer suffers pangs of conscience for not sharing his experiences with the colleagues he has left behind in his country. This anguish is linked with a heroic self-image; it is hardly ever possible, Miłosz concludes, to create a morally valuable work and at the same time to retain an unblemished image of oneself.

These, in Miłosz's opinion, are the sorrows of exile. Is it only the writer in exile who struggles with such difficulties? Are his colleagues, writing in their own language and moving in a world they have known since childhood, in a better situation? Are they really read and understood? Has not writing become in the contemporary world an exercise for lonely people, a signal sent out by the disinherited? The ultimate test of a writer's achievement, what decides his true standing in literature, his place in the community of writers, is the power of his language. Can his language maintain and develop sufficient force to be effective in a foreign setting? The answer from one of the privileged witnesses of these processes—Czesław Miłosz—is "yes." It is not true, he says, that prolonged residence abroad leads to impoverishment of style. It is true, however, that new aspects and tonalities of one's native language are revealed, that while the language may become impoverished in certain areas (the day-to-day speech of the streets or dialects), in others it becomes strengthened and purified. Anyone who comes into contact with Miłosz's poetry or Gombrowicz's prose will agree with this judgment. This is the most important conclusion from this conversation about the sorrows and the joys of writing in exile. That is how things might be, that is how they sometimes are. One has to pay a price for success. Nor is there any guarantee of success: that, too, is made clear by both the Polish writers in exile whose conversation I have tried to reconstruct here.

Tomas Venclova

An Exercise in Futility:
The Case of Andrei
Kurbsky

————

          I am from Lithuania, and
my paper may well turn out to be a continuation of this Eastern
European paranoia, but I really cannot help it. I hope that, at least in
part, it will provide an answer to Anton Shammas's question about
literature fighting totalitarianism or tyranny, and the hopelessness of
such a struggle.

    Sometimes I feel that all the countries of the world should be
divided into two large classes: the immigrant countries and the emigrant countries. Perhaps this is an oversimplification explained by
my own condition as a member of both those categories. But I would
defend my view. Everybody knows that America—her might, her
prosperity, her culture—has been created mainly, if not exclusively,
by the huddled masses yearning to breathe free (to paraphrase the
inscription on the Statue of Liberty). And vice versa. The culture of
Russia—though not her undeniable might and her nonexistent prosperity—has been created, almost to the same extent, by her émigrés,
by the wretched refuse of the teeming shore of that ancient and
pompous empire. Virtually the same applies to Poland, or for that
matter, to my native Lithuania, to all those lands of that ill-defined
realm called Eastern (or, sometimes, Central) Europe which remains
within the empire's reach. There are at least two kinds of such
émigrés. Some of them leave their countries for good, like Adam
Mickiewicz and Alexander Herzen in the nineteenth century, like

Czesław Miłosz and Joseph Brodsky in our own times. Others become so-called internal émigrés, like Boris Pasternak and Mikhail Bulgakov.

"Internal emigration" is a peculiar concept. Even Alexander Pushkin was an internal émigré, and to a considerable degree. He was more than eager to go abroad; predictably, he never managed to obtain permission. Driven to despair, he cherished such outlandish projects as joining the Russian delegation which was to visit Peking, and he even tried to enlist in the Russian army during the war with Turkey, just to put his foot on foreign soil. In that he succeeded: but the soil of the occupied part of Turkey, as he noted with some dismay, had already become Russian.

Many people have crossed the border line between such internal emigration and real emigration, sometimes in both directions. Among them were Marina Tsvetaeva and Sergei Prokofiev, for both of whom the experience proved, to put it mildly, traumatic. One has to admit that the border line between either of these types of emigration and death looks blurred.

There is a difference between mere tyranny and a hopeless tyranny. The latter is marked by total isolation and enclosure (the Marquis de Sade knew a lot about it). Countries that permanently close their borders create impressive mythologies to support that decision. These mythologies have been disproved hundreds of times. Nevertheless they have an immense potential for survival, not only through the governments' efforts, but also, as it were, through the force of common consent. The usual argument goes like this: the abandonment of one's society (or even the choice of internal emigration) is the equivalent of spiritual suicide. It is an act of treason comparable to adultery, or better still, to the betrayal of one's mother. It is a religious crime, a rejection of true Orthodoxy. Emigration means renouncement of certain mystical truths that can flourish only on one's native soil. Well, life on that soil is hard, one cannot deny that, but it is immoral and vicious to forsake one's country in her eternal misfortunes. A person cannot survive outside his native landscape. A writer cannot survive outside his native language. A human being is not just a human being endowed with reason and dignity, but part and parcel of his soil, a drop of his motherland's blood, a cogwheel in its spiritual mechanism. There is no reason and no dignity outside the collective soul of the people. A person is an embryo which cannot live after the cutting of the umbilical cord that joins him or her to the warm and mighty body of the Big Mother. An individual does not exist at all: it is as simple as that.

Of course there were people who rejected this mythology, either consciously or unconsciously. At least, they struggled against it, just as Jacob struggled with the angel. Arguably, the very best part of the Russian and East European culture originated as a result of that struggle and that rejection.

One could tell innumerable stories about such people, stories that, though not always amusing, are usually instructive. When Boris Godunov, a relatively liberal Tsar of the early seventeenth century (defamed by Pushkin in his well-known play), decided to send a dozen or so Russian youths belonging to noble families abroad to study, none of them came back. To quote Osip Mandelstam, the reason for that was very elementary: there is no way back from being into non-being. As far as I know, the experience of being proved unbearable, at least for some of them. Every day one of those young men approached the London palace where the Muscovite legation had its headquarters, and shouted, at a safe distance: "All of you in Muscovy are damned fools." Later he committed a theft and was duly hanged, in accordance with the English law. Unfortunately, this is one of the eternal paradigms of the fate of Russian and East European émigrés.

Much later, in the nineteenth century, there was a poet and philosopher of minor but unquestionable talent, whose name was Vladimir Pecherin. When sent by the authorities on a trip to Europe, he defected; moreover, he converted to Catholicism, became a Redemptorist monk and died in Dublin, of all places, having reached the advanced age of seventy-eight. In his later years he held extremely conservative views and arranged a public burning of the books he considered heretical (an act which caused a great scandal). There is a theory that he served as the model for the "Grand Inquisitor" in *The Brothers Karamazov*. Two of his lines deserve to be remembered:

How sweet it is to hate one's motherland,
Longing avidly for its annihilation.

This is, I agree, one of the more unusual—perhaps even more abominable—texts of world literature. But it forces me to worry less about Pecherin's depravity than about the nature of a motherland capable of inspiring such lines.

The longest story I am going to tell is a different one. The hero of that story was, beyond any doubt, less bizarre than Vladimir Pecherin and more mature than the hapless youth who perished in seventeenth-century London. He was a warrior, a statesman, and a good, if not particularly brilliant, writer. Moreover, he had the advantage of being the very first among the Russian exiles: the first who was bold enough to cut his umbilical cord, to become a separate human being and not just a particle of the collective soul. More than four hundred years separate us from him. His name was Prince Andrei Kurbsky. In a sense, he was and still is the patron of us all: not a patron saint (a saint he never was), but an ancestor; a man who faced most of our problems and sometimes even spoke our language.

The story, to be precise, has two heroes. The second is an even more remarkable man. He was the Tsar of All Russia, the first to use the title "Tsar," which meant emperor. In the Western tradition, he is commonly known as Ivan the Terrible. This is an inaccurate translation of the Russian "Ivan Grozny," since *grozny* means stern and formidable. The adjective is often used to describe one's father, a force of nature or some deity. It was also more often than not applied to Stalin. According to a generally held opinion, it meant that the ruler, while threatening, was at the same time rather benevolent toward his loyal subjects. Let us call him here Ivan the Stern.

His reign was truly spectacular, even by Russian standards. Only Stalin exceeded Ivan the Stern in the range of his enterprise: but Stalin had trains, machine guns, and modern media at his disposal. Ivan subjugated Tartars and many other tribes, making Russia for the first time in history into a multinational state (which she remains to this very day). He rejected—once and forever—any concept of territorial or personal autonomy in his country. He limited the power of the nobility, mainly by means of physical elimination. He organized the *oprichnina*, a sort of KGB *avant la lettre*, which tortured and killed alleged traitors by the thousands, more often than not in Ivan's presence. He led his army against the proud and beautiful city of Novgorod, which he wrongly suspected of intending to secede from the state, and ordered his *oprichniki* to drown most of its inhabitants in the ice holes in the Volkhov river. During Ivan's reign, to be appointed head of any central department was an invitation to a beheading; it is easy to comprehend that the *oprichniki* themselves enjoyed no immunity. Ivan forced some of his supposed enemies to denounce themselves and then to take poison. In a fit of madness he killed his son, the only one with some ability for governing (the other one was good-natured and imbecilic). Moreover, he started a war with the Polish-Lithuanian Commonwealth and with Sweden that lasted twenty-four years and was almost as senseless as the Iran-Iraq war.

I suspect that many, if not all, the people of Moscow actually loved him. They gave him dictatorial powers, and he never grew tired of praising their loyalty and patience, just as Stalin did four hundred years later. Strangely enough, Ivan displayed warm feelings toward England as well. He offered Queen Elizabeth the right of mutual political asylum in case of an emergency. He even thought of marrying her. One can only hazard the wildest guesses about the possible influence of such a remarkable marriage on the fate of mankind. And there were some Englishmen among the *oprichniki*: the likes of Mr. Kim Philby are never in short supply.

Ivan's last years were even more astonishing in that he "rehabilitated" posthumously all of his victims and ordered the church to pray for their souls. That way, he performed the formidable feat of combining Stalin, Khrushchev, and Gorbachev in one person. His total lack of responsibility to God, or history, or both, had brought his country to the verge of total disaster (it took approximately one hundred years for Russia to come to her senses, partly to be sure, after Ivan the Stern). Some historians, Soviet and non-Soviet, tend to absolve Ivan of his numerous sins, pointing to the fact that he abolished outdated feudal customs and became, in all practical senses, the founder of the modern Russian state. That brings us to an old question: Is modern always good? I think most of Ivan's subjects would have had a very definite answer to that question.

Like many dictators, Ivan had a weakness for playing chess, and it proved fatal: he died, presumably in a fit of anger, when one of his partners dared to win a game. At that time, he was fifty-four, and a very old man. No wonder.

Prince Andrei Kurbsky, two years older than Ivan, did not live long enough to see Ivan's death. He grew up virtually in the same milieu as the future Tsar (they were relatives, and not too distant ones). The fates of both were closely interconnected. Kurbsky took part in some of Ivan's administrative reforms and in some of his wars; he served with distinction and was ruthless enough to earn the Tsar's confidence and friendship. Then something happened. During the war with the Polish-Lithuanian Commonwealth Kurbsky fell out of favor. Perhaps he displayed some sympathy with the executed and ruined, many of whom were his friends and relatives; perhaps he was irritated by the obvious senselessness of the war in which he was obliged to take part; perhaps his tastes were slightly too conservative for him to enjoy Ivan's paranoid innovations. In any event, he became an internal émigré. He had little choice but to scheme and to defect since Ivan the Stern suspected everybody of intending to defect, and of scheming. But virtually all the suspects remained in Russia, out of loyalty to Ivan and to their country: some perished, some did not. One may assume that in Kurbsky's case there was an additional, perhaps a subconscious, factor: he had to follow his vocation. He was born to be a writer, and today we remember him mainly in that capacity. He was fond of Cicero and Saint John Chrysostom (he translated both of them), and he was rather interested in books and Western ideas. Yet there was no place for a writer in Ivan's Russia, except, of course, for Ivan himself. In 1564, therefore, Kurbsky left "God's land." He crossed the border with a large crowd of adherents and servants and arrived in Lithuania. He was thirty-six.

There is much irony in Kurbsky's fate. To me, the first irony is that the free world of those olden days which welcomed him was my native country. For almost two centuries (except for a short and precarious period of independence during the twenties and thirties) Lithuania, in popular opinion at least, was and is part of the Russian empire. Nowadays she shares Russia's fate and has to conform to the Russian way of life, even if very reluctantly. Here one cannot but recall the inexorable growth of evil (or the so-called inexorable course of history described and praised by Karl Marx). During the medieval and the Renaissance periods Lithuania was a great nation (larger than Russia itself), maintaining a union with Poland, but fiercely protecting her independence, a democracy by the standards of the age, quite prosperous and moderately corrupt (to quote Czesław Miłosz). Russian was widely spoken there, together with Lithuanian, Polish, Latin, German, and several other languages. In short, Lithuania, for any of the subjects of Ivan the Stern, looked very much like the United States to a Soviet émigré of nowadays. And Kurbsky's story looks like a typical story of a successful defector. He was granted political asylum; he was debriefed by the intelligence service of the Polish-Lithuanian Commonwealth (a rather modest institution, at that time), and presented some sensitive information on Ivan's character and intentions; he was given an office and several large estates. (His mother, his wife and his only son had perished in Ivan's prisons. His brothers were murdered, and their considerable wealth was distributed among the *oprichniki*: that was the normal procedure). Then, Prince Andrei Kurbsky started to write.

His abundant literary work includes historical essays, translations of the lives of the saints and a theological treatise. But his main task and life's goal was to settle accounts with Ivan the Stern and with the Russia that Kurbsky had been forced to leave. He badly needed to comprehend what had happened to him, and to the Tsar, and to their country. Perhaps he attempted to rationalize his act as an exercise in the traditional freedom of a knight to choose his sovereign. At the same time, he could not help but grasp that he had done something new and unusual: he had deliberately left his land and the realm of strict Orthodoxy. That was threatening, and—perhaps—led to an irretrievable loss of identity. The pain was particularly acute since Kurbsky was a traditionalist (while Ivan was a modernist). For Kurbsky, the process of reaching one of the first modern decisions in Russia's history became an unbearable burden.

He dispatched to Ivan a short letter, the first surviving document of Russian dissent and of Russian émigré prose. He wrote in a heavily rhetorical fashion, quoting the Bible and Cicero, but one can discern a faint flicker of a new and personal language under that traditional guise—a language adequate to the unique historical challenge Kurbsky had to face.

> Wherefore, O Tsar, have you destroyed the strong in Israel and subjected to various forms of death the *voyevodas* given to you by God? And wherefore have you spilt their victorious, holy blood in the churches of God during sacerdotal ceremonies, and stained the thresholds of the churches with their martyred blood? . . . At the head of your army have I marched, and no

dishonor have I brought upon you . . . and this, not in one year, not yet in two—but throughout many years have I toiled with much sweat and patience; and always have I been separated from my fatherland, and little have I seen my parents, and my wife have I not known; but always in far-distant towns have I stood in arms against your foes and I have suffered many wants and natural illnesses, of which my Lord Jesus Christ is witness. . . . But to you, O Tsar, was all this as nought; rather do you show us your intolerable wrath and most bitter hatred, and, furthermore, burning stoves.

[The burning stove was a form of torture of which Ivan was particularly fond; the translation is by John Fennell.—ed.]

Ivan deemed it necessary to answer the traitor, and did it without delay. He wrote a very long and vigorous letter, later characterized by Kurbsky as a "grandiloquent and big-sounding screed." A dramatic correspondence ensued. It makes, beyond any doubt, one of the most interesting books ever written in Russian. While reading it, one notices a new ironical turn: Ivan was a much better writer than his adversary. Of course, both of them were helped by scribes, but Ivan's personality shows itself on every page. There is a sort of Shakespearean quality in him: he is passionate and witty, sincere and hypocritical, erudite and totally idiosyncratic; in short, he is extremely individualistic (no wonder, since he was the only human being in his empire allowed to be an individual).

His speech is a magnificent dramatic performance: mocking, taunting, tantalizing, complaining, bewitching. All the devices described by the Russian formalists are already there. (If I may be permitted a facile pun, Ivan the Stern was almost as bizarre an author as Lawrence Sterne.) He postures and changes masks. His curses are virtually untranslatable, though seldom obscene. Of course, the motivating power beyond that astonishing performance was paranoia and fear of death: Ivan the Stern knew death rather intimately and kept up a lifelong love-hate relation with it.

Kurbsky-the-writer pales in comparison: he is less original, less bold, and never totally sure of his right to act the way he did. His prose is languid, sometimes dull, and over the course of years more and more tainted by half-digested Polonisms. To make things worse,

Ivan usually sounds much more convincing, drawing (he—a modernist) upon the ancient Biblical, Byzantine, and Russian traditions for ready-made ideas and patterns of thought. The-world-according-to-Ivan became intrinsically evil after the First Fall. It is built on blood, hierarchy and bitter duty. A reasonable ruler chosen by God must introduce a measure of order into that evil world by every means at his disposal: "And we are free to reward our servants, and we are also free to punish them. . . . Dogs are executed in all countries."

And Kurbsky, the conservative and the traditionalist, groped awkwardly for something not firmly rooted in that ancient tradition. He attempted to say that forcible oaths and hierarchies cannot bind a human being; that execution without due process is not divine justice; that one should not praise one's native country while it is a prison, even less so while it is a torture chamber; that one cannot love one's homeland if one cannot leave it and return at will. He himself never became totally convinced that these strange truths amounted to more than "Polish barbarism." That was his fatal weakness, and one more irony of his botched life.

His last years were less than happy. He liked Latin and spoke Polish, but at the same time he fiercely denounced Catholic influences upon the "pure" Slavonic language and literature: that is, he made every effort to remain within the realm of true orthodoxy, from which he had excluded himself by defection. He considered his era an Age of the Beast and was fond of apocalyptic prophesies. It was no accident that he earned fame as one of the most violent nobles of his new country, which itself was never short of unpredictable men. His second marriage was disastrous. He maliciously enjoyed armed attacks on his neighbors and dozens of ensuing legal disputes. His sergeants and policemen mistreated Jews (a practice unusual in the sixteenth-century Commonwealth). He suffered endless humiliations, underpayment, deceit: his new homeland, although only moderately corrupt, was rather good in the art of petty harassment. When approached by the king's envoys, he used to heap on them "vile Muscovite curses," yielding only to Ivan in this field. A broken and impoverished man, he died at the age of fifty-five—one year before his adversary.

And now, the ultimate irony: a Harvard scholar, Edward L. Keenan, declared in 1971 that all the correspondence between Kurbsky and Ivan was apocryphal. Supported by sophisticated textological analyses, Keenan claims it was a fake concocted by a certain Semyon Shakhovskoy, who lived about one hundred years later. Semyon Shakhovskoy was a writer in his own right, and he had ample, if complex, reasons for his alleged forgery. A lively controversy arose. It is still going on, though it seems that, at present, Keenan's opponents are gaining the upper hand. I personally have never been convinced by Keenan's argument. In my opinion, it violates an old rule of scholarly methodology known as "Ockham's razor." The rule states that the simplest of competing theories is to be preferred to the more complex ones: and it is much simpler to believe that Kurbsky and Ivan wrote their letters themselves than to muse over Shakhovskoy's possible actions, his intricate reasons and his amazing ability to create two totally different literary personae. But I cannot fail to note the sad humor of the situation. Here is an exile whose life's goal was to make some sense out of his predicament, and along comes posterity, which will never be totally sure that he did what he did.

Therefore our story is as absurd as many other stories about exile. Prince Kurbsky, the forefather of all Russian, and not only Russian, dissidents and émigrés, was a loser, and this cannot be helped. His letters to Ivan were an exercise in futility. Nothing changed and nothing could have been changed in Ivan's Russia by those letters. Even the country where Kurbsky found shelter is today but a part of Ivan's empire. Moreover, even in purely literary terms, Kurbsky's adversary won the battle. Then, to heap insult on injury, Kurbsky's life work—in a sense, his very existence—has been put in doubt by a new generation, four hundred years after his death. Virtually nothing can be said in his favor, except the insignificant fact that he was right. He went against the common opinion of his times, and that is what writing is all about. He was Andrei Kurbsky. And Ivan the Stern was Ivan the Terrible.

Yuri Druzhnikov

Report of a New Arrival

▬▬▬

[Introduction] It gives me pleasure to introduce to you a new member of our society, Mr. Yuri Druzhnikov, who was in an extremely difficult situation in Moscow when last we saw him. He comes directly from the internal emigration to the outer emigration. He has now been in the West for two months. Hopefully, life will be better for him here.—Lev Kopelev

I am a newcomer to the West, and with time I may well change many of my opinions and begin to sing a quite different tune. However, although I find your experience very interesting, the fact is that I actually emigrated spiritually long ago. Regrettably, my trip from Moscow to Vienna took ten years, two hours, and thirty-two minutes.

I am sure your life stories (and I am already acquainted with some of them—especially those of the Russian writers) are considerably more exciting than mine, but mine is unusual in that it has to do with the literary aspects of *glasnost*. I myself was a victim of the absence of *glasnost*, and then of *glasnost* itself.

My conflict with the Soviet authorities began ten years ago—over certain moral aspects of the Soviet educational system. The upshot of the matter was a decision, on my part, to emigrate. Many of you ran into similar dead-ends. My situation was unusual in that I was expelled from all the literary institutions—secretly, so that neither my colleagues nor I knew of the fact. My three manuscripts disappeared from the publishing houses, my plays were withdrawn from the theater repertoire, and then I was informed that I wouldn't be allowed to emigrate. Of course, I started publishing my writings abroad.

Then came the break between the older and the younger generation of Soviet leaders; it was the beginning of the era of *glasnost*. The KGB called me in for questioning, and I was warned that my short stories and essays published abroad, and even my telegram to Academician Sakharov on the occasion of his sixtieth birthday, were anti-Soviet propaganda which poisoned the bright period of *glasnost*. They said there were only two paths for a person like me: one led to a psychiatric institution and the other to a forced-labor camp. I was not permitted to publish, and I was not permitted to emigrate.

In the tenth year of my internal exile I finished a new manuscript, which I began to distribute clandestinely, in keeping with the new spirit of *glasnost*. I wrote an open letter to the members of the Soviet Writers' Union: they publish writers who are already dead, I wrote, but what about me? Would I have to wait to die to be published? I made 450 copies and sent it to all the top organizations, but there was no answer. I remained a "nonwriter."

Since the Americans were scheduled to participate in the Moscow Book Fair, we decided to have a last try. We declared that we were going to open an alternative writers' union in the Soviet Union—for those who had been expelled from the official Writers' Union. We were going to call it the "Authors' Union." In addition we intended to take literally the promises of *glasnost* and *perestroika* and found a private publishing house called the "Golden Cockerel." The day before our undertaking was to have been launched we received a call from the visa office. It was the deputy chief of the Moscow office himself: "Why are you so nervous?" he asked. "You can pick up your visas."

Do you think I am here as a result of my struggle, or as a result of *glasnost*? No, I think I am a victim again. The biggest surprise I have found here in Vienna is the West's desire to support Gorbachev in *glasnost*. They want to help him stay in power. The view has been expressed that there are writers in exile who are afraid of *glasnost* and that there would be an open dialogue between obedient writers and émigré writers, but as a historian I would compare *glasnost* not to the Thaw, but to a *smuta*, a Time of Troubles. We have had many of these in Russia. Russian history can be divided into three, quite clear periods: three hundred years under the Tartar-Mongol yoke, three hundred years under the Romanovs, and three hundred years under the Bolsheviks. The latter have celebrated only their seventieth anniversary in power, so it seems to me that we Russian writers here and all over the world will have a lot of time to speak our minds.

Dennis Brutus   I would like to suggest one very specific area in which we, as exiles, might be able to ease the predicament of other exiles. "Charter 87" was recently launched in Westminster Abbey with a very distinguished list of endorsers from many fields—art, writing, theater, music, and, of course, politics. The clergy was represented by the archbishop of Canterbury, the chief rabbi, and the Catholic cardinal in Britain.

What they are trying to do through Charter 87 seems to me in some ways a sequel to what was attempted in Charter 77—to address the predicament of the exile with an appeal for international cooperation in easing the process of exile.

Nuruddin Farah   The difference between a refugee and an exile seems to be that a refugee is someone who has "no economic or financial support," while an exile *probably* (a) is of middle-class background, (b) writes, and (c) has a second job with which to support himself. So I am delighted to take note of the two previous speakers, who have brought to our attention the plight of millions and millions of refugees all over the world, and I suggest that we try to do something practical to help them.

Jaroslav Vejvoda   Ladies and gentlemen, we have reached the end of the conference, and I would again like to raise the delicate topic which I mentioned yesterday of the mass flight of hundreds of thousands and even millions of people in today's world, people who, unlike us, cannot use words to defend themselves. These are people who have no lobby, and who are largely ignored.

I would like to begin with a tragicomic story. The film director Bernard Šafarik is a friend and compatriot of mine. Three years ago the two of us produced a film in Switzerland—a film which is based on a true-life story. It is the story of a refugee, quite by chance from Czechoslovakia. After months of petitioning for refugee status, his request was rejected, and he was put on a Czechoslovak plane in chains and deported back to the Czechoslovakian Socialist Republic. His subsequent fate is unknown to us. We had no way of finding out.

We all know quite well that "flight from the republic" is considered a crime in all the countries of Eastern Europe. The Swiss officials, like officials in all the other Western European countries, refused to recognize him as a refugee because he had not formerly been politically active (he was very young), but had simply refused to return while in the West as a tourist. However, he is probably now in prison as a political refugee.

We were not able to do anything for him, so we decided to use this film to try to gain public attention, even if we could not hope for great numbers.

The incident took place in 1984; the film was made in 1985 and was being shown in Swiss movie theaters in 1986, when the same thing happened just around the corner in Zurich to a Polish refugee. The Zurich police, now famous (or perhaps infamous) as a result of Remarque's novel *Love Thy Neighbor*, deported the young Pole back to Warsaw in the very same fashion. I doubt that the police go to movies, but in this particular instance we could boast of a small achievement: the police apologized after a fashion and classified the man's act as an error. In any case, he could not be helped any further.

But these are individual cases. There are thousands of people who are forced either to return "voluntarily"—and perhaps end up in prison—or to take their families and live illegally. I know of similar cases in Norway. There were three hundred Yugoslavs who requested political asylum, but who were nevertheless forcibly deported back to Yugoslavia.

I do not share the political views of the Albanians in Yugoslavia, but I must assume that these are people in real danger, who are nevertheless sent back.

What can we do? It is hardly the task of literature to interfere directly in politics. My famous compatriot Milan Kundera likes to quote the words of the Central European and Austrian, Herman Broch, who said, more or less, that there is no morality in literature.

The only moral duty of the novel is to reveal a new aspect of life. I approve these words, but I do not believe that we have the right to evade this problem and to remain silent.

I would like to close with a remark made in a bar by another even more famous compatriot, Joseph Schweik, about the telephone operator on the Titanic who kept calling the ship's kitchen—even as the ship was sinking—and asking if supper was ready. These are questions which we must all ask ourselves. Do you remember the telephone operator?

Glossary of Names

If the writer is known by a pseudonym, the real name is indicated in parentheses. If the writer uses an abbreviated form of his or her name, the full name is given in parentheses.

Akhmatova, Anna (1888–1966). Russian poet.

Aksyonov, Vasily (b. 1932). Russian novelist forced to emigrate in 1980 after participating in the publication of a nonofficial literary almanac entitled *Metropol*. Lives in Washington, D.C.

Arrabal, Fernando (b. 1932). French playwright born in Morocco. Writes in the Theater of the Absurd tradition.

Baldwin, James (1924–1987). Black American novelist, essayist and playwright. Lived chiefly in France. Best known for his novel *Another Country*.

Balzac, Honoré de (1799–1850). Generally considered to be the greatest nineteenth-century French novelist.

Barre, Muhammad Siyad (b. 1919). President of Somalia, seized power in a military coup in which elected President Abdirashid Ali Shermarke was assassinated.

Baudelaire, Charles (1821–1867). French poet, critic, novelist, and playwright.

Beckett, Samuel Barclay (b. 1906). Irish, Nobel Prize-winning playwright and novelist who has lived in Paris since 1937. Writes absurdist comedy, mainly in French.

Ben Jelloun, Tahar (b. 1944). Moroccan poet, novelist, and essayist. Writes in French.

Benjamin, Walter (1892–1940). German-Jewish man of letters and aesthetician who left Germany for France in 1933. Informed by the police that he would be turned over to the Gestapo, he committed suicide.

Blok, Alexander (1880–1921). Russian Symbolist poet. Most famous work: *The Twelve*, a longish mystical poem about the Russian revolution.

Brecht, Bertolt (1898–1956). German dramatist, poet, and theatrical producer. After Hitler came to power in 1933, Brecht went into self-imposed exile in Scandinavia and the United States. Settled in East Germany after World War II.

Broch, Herman (1886–1951). Austrian novelist, novella and short-story writer, essayist, and dramatist. After a brief imprisonment in 1938, Broch was permitted to emigrate to the United States, via England and Scotland.

Bulgakov, Mikhail (1891–1940). Russian novelist, short-story writer, and dramatist. Best known for his novel *The Master and Margarita*.

Burtin, Yu. Author of an article, published in a Soviet journal, on a 1969 anti-Stalinist poem by poet and editor Alexander Tvardovsky, which was suppressed by the censors and which Burtin sees as relevant to Soviet readers today. See " 'Vam, iz drugogo pokoleniya,' " *Oktyabr'*, 1987, No. 8, 191–202.

Čapek, Karel (1890–1938). Czech novelist, dramatist, and short-story writer. Best known for his antiutopias *R.U.R.* (Rossum's Universal Robots) and *War with the Newts*.

Carpentier y Valmont, Arejo (1940–1980). Cuban novelist, short-story writer, and poet. Lived in Paris for many years.

Casals, Pablo (1876–1973). Spanish cellist, conductor, and composer. Outspoken opponent of fascism. Refused to return to Spain after the Spanish Civil War of 1936–1939.

Celan, Paul (pseudonym of Paul Antschel) (1920–1970). Born in Rumania of Hasidic Jewish heritage. Lyric poet who wrote in German, often about the Holocaust.

Cernuda y Bidón, Luis (1902–1963). Spanish poet and critic. On a tour of Britain in 1938, he refused to return home after the fall of the Spanish Republic. Later moved to the United States, and then to Mexico.

Chrysostom, Saint John (347–407). Appointed archbishop of Constantinople in 398. Enjoyed a stormy term in office and was exiled to Armenia. An important theologian who kept up a lively correspondence with supporters.

Cioran, Emil Michel (b. 1911). Rumanian essayist who writes chiefly in French. Permanently domiciled in France since 1947.

Coetzee, John M. (b. 1940). South African novelist whose books focus on the underprivileged.

Comenius (secular name of Jan Amos Komensky) (1592–1670). Evangelical priest forced into exile by the Counter-Reformation and invasion of the Spanish army.

Conrad, Joseph (pseudonym of Teodor Josef Korzeniowski) (1857–1924). Polish-born English novelist.

Dante Alighieri (1265–1321). Italian poet. Author of *The Divine Comedy*. While in Rome in 1302, Dante was condemned in absentia to be burned at the stake in his native Florence and thus was forced to remain in exile.

Dürrenmatt, Friedrich (b. 1921). Swiss novelist, playwright, and painter.

Ellison, Ralph (b. 1914). Black American novelist, short-story writer, and essayist. His first novel, *Invisible Man*, received the National Book Award in 1952.

Etkind, Yefim (b. 1918). Russian critic, translator, and literary historian. In 1974 he was stripped of academic degrees and positions for dissident activities. Emigrated to France in 1974.

Fitzgerald, F(rancis) Scott (1896–1940). American novelist, short-story writer, and scenarist. Viewed as a spokesman for the "jazz age." Best known work: *The Great Gatsby*.

Fleming, Ian Lancaster (1908–1964). British adventure writer; creator of James Bond.

Gide, André (pseudonym of Paul Guillaume) (1869–1951). French novelist, essayist, poet, and dramatist. Received the Nobel Prize in literature in 1947.

Ginsberg, Allen (b. 1926). American poet of the "beat" generation.

Gladilin, Anatoly (b. 1935). Russian writer and essayist. Published in *samizdat* and the West. Emigrated in 1976 and settled in France.

Goethe, Johann Wolfgang (1749–1832). German poet, prose writer, and thinker. Author of *Faust*.

Gogol, Nikolai (1809–1852). Expatriate Russian novelist and dramatist who settled in Italy. Best known for his comic play "The Inspector General" and novel *Dead Souls*.

Gombrowicz, Witold (1904–1969). Polish novelist best known for *Ferdydurke* and *Pornografia*.

Goytisolo, Juan (b. 1931). Spanish novelist who has lived in France since 1957.

Grani. Russian émigré journal founded in 1946 in Frankfurt-am-Main. Associated with the "People's Labor Union" (Narodno-trudovoi soyuz), an anti-Soviet political organization.

Griboyedov, Alexander (1794 or 1795–1829). Russian writer and diplomat most known for his satirical play *Woe from Wit*. Killed during uprising in Teheran.

Havel, Václav (b. 1936). Czech dramatist, essayist, and poet. Associated with Prague's avant-garde theater of the 1960s. In 1979 sentenced to four and a half years in prison for allegedly subversive activities.

Hemingway, Ernest Miller (1899–1961). American novelist and short-story writer. Winner of Pulitzer and Nobel prizes. Committed suicide.

Herzen, Alexander (1812–1870). Russian novelist, essayist, and short-story writer. Emigrated to Europe in 1846 and settled in England in 1852. Best known for his memoirs, *My Past and Thoughts*.

Hikmet, Nâzim (Nâzim Hikmet Ran) (1902–1963). Turkish poet, dramatist, novelist, and short-story writer. Replaced the conventional stanzaic form and rhyme patterns of Turkish poetry with free verse. Spent fifteen years in Turkish prison for Communist views and moved to the Soviet Union, where he died.

Hugo, Victor (1802–1885). French Romantic writer. In 1851, he left France for twenty years.

Huidobro, Fincente (Fincente García Huidobro Fernández) (1893–1948). Chilean poet, novelist, and essayist. Formulated "Creationism," in which he equated poetry with absolute creation. Spent all but one year from 1912 to 1945 outside Chile.

Hus, Jan (1369–1415). Czech priest and theologist, and a follower of the religious beliefs of John Wycliffe, who attacked the doctrine of Papal Supremacy, celibacy for priests, and the doctrine of transubstantiation. Burned at the stake.

Ibsen, Henrik Johan (1828–1906). Norwegian playwright, essayist, and poet. Often called "the father of modern drama." Lived outside Norway for almost thirty years.

Ionesco, Eugène (b. 1912). Rumanian-born French dramatist, essayist, script writer, and novelist. Best known as a dramatist linked to the Theater of the Absurd.

Iskander, Fazil (b. 1929). Russian-Abkhazian poet and prose writer.

Jakobson, Roman (1896–1982). Russian linguist and literary scholar. Emigrated to Czechoslovakia in 1921, and later to the United States, where he was a professor at Harvard University.

Jiménez, Juan Ramón (Juan Ramón Jiménez Mantécon) (1881–1958). Nobel Prize-winning Spanish poet.

Joyce, James (Augustine Aloysius) (1882–1941). Irish prose writer, poet, and dramatist. Best known for his novel *Ulysses*.

Jünger, Ernst (b. 1895). German novelist and essayist, former ardent militarist who became an equally ardent believer in peace after his son died fighting in Italy during World War II. Indirectly involved in plot to kill Hitler.

Kafka, Franz (1883–1924). Austro-Czech novelist, short-story writer, and diarist. Best known work: *The Trial* (published posthumously).

Kandinsky, Vasily (1866–1944). Russian abstract artist who emigrated to Germany in 1896. Founder of the Munich group "Der blaue Reiter."

Kartashov, Anton (1875–1960). Russian professor of church history. Fled Russia in 1919 and settled in Paris.

Karyakin, Yury. Author of an article in a Soviet journal responding to an anonymous letter attacking a recent novel by B. Mozhaev. Karyakin accuses the author of the letter of slander and views him as representative of the Soviet establishment in the post-Stalinist period up to Gorbachev. See "Stoit li nastupat' na grabli?" *Znamya*, 1987, No. 9, 200–224.

Kerensky, Alexander (1881–1970). Head of the Russian Provisional Government in 1917. Emigrated to France in 1918 and from there to the United States in 1940.

Khazanov, Boris (pseudonym of Gennady Faibusovich). Russian novelist, short-story writer, and essayist. Sentenced to forced labor in 1949 for "anti-Soviet propaganda." Emigrated to Germany in 1982 and edits Russian émigré magazine *Strana i mir* (The Country and the World).

Koestler, Arthur (1905–1983). Hungarian-born British writer, best known for his novel *Darkness at Noon*.

Košinski, Jerzy Nikodem (b. 1933). Polish-born novelist who now resides in the United States. Best known for his novel *The Painted Bird*.

Kotoshikhin, Grigory (1630?–1667). Russian writer who, for having incorrectly copied out the title of Tsar Aleksey Mikhailovich, was beaten with rods. Later fled to Sweden, where he was found guilty of murder and executed.

Kundera, Milan (b. 1929). Nobel Prize-winning Czech novelist and short-story writer. His work was banned in Czechoslovakia in 1967.

Le Pen, Jean-Marie (b. 1928). French political figure seeking to limit immigration to France.

Lermontov, Mikhail (1814–1841). Romantic Russian poet and novelist. Killed in duel.

Lezama Lima, José (1910–1976). Cuban poet, novelist, and essayist out of favor with the Castro regime.

Ligachev, Yegor (b. 1920). Member of Soviet Politburo who often opposes *glasnost* (openness) and *perestroika* (restructuring) under Gorbachev.

Lohengrin. Mysterious knight in German legends of the Middle Ages who arrives—in a boat drawn by a swan—to help a noble lady in distress. He marries her, but forbids her to ask his origin. She later forgets this promise, and he leaves her, never to return.

Mácha, Karel Hynek (1810–1836). Romantic Czech poet and novelist.

Mailer, Norman (b. 1923). American novelist and social critic, best known for his novel *The Naked and the Dead*.

Maksimov, Vladimir (pseudonym of Lev Samsonov). Russian novelist. Expelled from the Soviet Writers' Union in 1973 for publishing in the West. Emigrated in 1974, where he edits the journal *Kontinent*.

Malaprop, Mrs. A character in R. B. Sheridan's 1775 novel *The Rivals*, known for her aptitude for misapplying long words.

Mandelstam, Osip (1891–1938). Russian "Acmeist" poet. Died in Soviet forced-labor camp.

Martí y Pérez, José Julián (1853–1895). Cuban poet and essayist, repeatedly exiled from Cuba for political activities. Died in battle after one month in the army of Cuban revolutionary leader Máximo Gómez.

Mickiewicz, Adam (1798–1855). Polish poet, dramatist, and novelist. Jailed in 1823 by the Russian government for alleged conspiracy and exiled to Russia for four years. Eventually he settled in France, never to return home.

Miller, Arthur (b. 1915). Pulitzer Prize-winning American playwright.

Miłosz, Czesław (b. 1911). Nobel Prize-winning Lithuanian poet now living in the United States. Writes primarily in Polish.

Musil, Robert (1880–1942). Austrian novelist, novella writer, dramatist, and poet. Fled to Switzerland with Jewish wife in 1938.

Nabokov, Vladimir (1899–1977). Russian-American novelist who lived outside of Russia since 1919. Switched from Russian to the English language.

Naipaul, V(idiadhar) S(urajprassad) (b. 1932). West Indian novelist, short-story writer, and author of travel books who has lived in England since 1950. Best known work: *A House for Mr. Biswas*.

Neizvestny, Ernst (b. 1926). Sculptor and artist who became known in the West after a 1962 quarrel with Khrushchev. Emigrated and settled in New York in 1976.

Němcová, Božena (1820–1862). Czech prose writer who wrote in epic style. Best known work: *Babička* (Grandmother).

Neruda, Pablo (1904–1973). Nobel Prize-winning Chilean poet.

Nesch, Rolf (1893–1975). German-Norwegian printmaker who worked in Expressionist, Surrealist, and abstract formats.

Okudzhava, Bulat (b. 1924). Soviet poet and novelist of Georgian-Armenian background who writes in Russian. Best known for his songs about Moscow life.

Ortega y Gasset, José (1883–1955). Spanish philosopher and essayist.

Ortiz, Fernando (1881–1969). Cuban anthropologist and theorist of the Afro-Cuban movement.

Orwell, George (pseudonym of Eric Arthur Blair) (1903–1950). British novelist and critic known for his antiutopias *Animal Farm* and *1984*.

Ovid (Publius Ovidius Naso) (43 B.C.–17 A.D.). Roman poet sent into exile by Augustus in 8 A.D.

Pasternak, Boris (1890–1960). Russian poet and novelist forced by the Soviet authorities to reject the Nobel Prize. Author of *Dr. Zhivago*.

Patočka, Jan (b. 1907). Czech philosopher who, under the influence of Husserl, attacked positivism.

Pecherin, Vladimir (1807–1885). Russian poet and thinker who left Russia in 1836 to live in England and Scotland. Abandoned utopian socialism to become a Redemptorist monk.

Rousseau, Henri (byname: Le Douanier—"the customs officer") (1844–1910). French painter, archetype of the naive artist.

Samoilov, David (pseudonym of David Kaufman) (b. 1920). Russian poet and translator.

Saroyan, William (1908–1981). Armenian-American novelist, short-story writer, and playwright.

Sartre, Jean-Paul (1905–1980). Nobel Prize-winning existential novelist.

Schönberg, Arnold (Franz Walter) (1874–1951). Austrian composer of Jewish background who created the twelve-tone method of composition (atonality). After the Nazis came to power in Germany in 1933, he emigrated to the United States.

Sholokhov, Mikhail (1905–1984). Russian writer who actively supported the Soviet government from Stalin to Brezhnev. Famous for one novel, *The Quiet Don*, for which he received the Nobel Prize. Some scholars believe the manuscript of the novel may have been stolen by Sholokhov from White officer Fyodor Kryukov.

Silone, Ignazio (1900–1978). Italian novelist best known for *Bread and Wine*, a fictional indictment of Italian fascism.

Sinyavsky, Andrei (occasional pseudonym: Abram Terts) (b. 1925). Russian prose writer, essayist and literary critic. Arrested with Yuly Daniel in 1965 for clandestine publication of literary compositions in the West. Emigrated in 1973 and settled in Paris.

Slutsky, Boris (b. 1919). Russian poet. In late 1950s and early 1960s some of his poems circulated in *samizdat*.

Sokolov, Sasha Alexander (b. 1943). Russian novelist known for his intricate style. Emigrated in 1975 and settled in the United States. Now a Canadian citizen.

Solzhenitsyn, Aleksandr (b. 1918). Russian novelist and historian. Himself a former inmate of Soviet forced-labor camps, Solzhenitsyn became famous when Khrushchev permitted publication of his short novel about life in the camps, *One Day in the Life of Ivan Denisovich*. Expelled from the USSR in 1969 and stripped of Soviet citizenship. Now a U.S. citizen.

Spiel, Hilde (b. 1911). Austrian novelist and journalist. Lived in Great Britain from 1936 to 1963.

Sosnora, Viktor (b. 1936). Russian poet keenly interested in old Russian literature.

Stein, Gertrude (1874–1946). American novelist, poet, critic, and playwright. Moved to France in 1903. Popular autobiography: *The Autobiography of Alice B. Toklas*.

Štoll, Ladislav (1902–1981). Czechoslovak establishment critic and specialist on Marxist aesthetics.

Stoppard, Tom (b. 1937). Czech-born playwright and novelist, now living in England. His best-known play is *Rosencrantz and Guildenstern Are Dead*.

Struve, Gleb (1898–1985). Russian émigré literary scholar who settled in California and wrote a book on Russian exile literature.

Svědectví. Czech émigré journal on politics and literature, founded in New York in 1955.

Tsvetaeva, Marina (1892–1941). One of Russia's two greatest women poets (the other is Anna Akhmatova). Fled from Russia in 1922, repatriated in 1939. Committed suicide.

Tzara, Tristan (pseudonym of Samuel Rosenfeld) (1896–1963). Rumanian-born French poet, dramatist and essayist. Proponent and theoretician of Dadaism.

Vaculík, Ludvik Alton (b. 1930). Poet and playwright born in the West Indies. Author of *In a Green Night* and *The Dream on Monkey Mountain.*

Wells, H(erbert) G(eorge) (1886–1946). English novelist, short-story writer, essayist, and historian. Together with Jules Verne, a founder of modern science fiction. His novel *The Invisible Man* was first published in 1897.

Wilder, Thornton Niven (1897–1975). American playwright and novelist. Won three Pulitzer Prizes.

Williams, Tennessee (1911–1983). American Southern playwright.

Woelfflin, Heinrich (1864–1945). Swiss art historian and aesthetician. Taught in Berlin and Munich from 1901 to 1924, then returned to Switzerland.

Wols, Wolfgang Schultze (1913–1951). German painter and graphic artist.

Yershov, Pyotr (1815–1869). Russian writer who composed fairy tales and verse.

Zhdanov, Andrei (1896–1948). Soviet political figure who organized the attacks on Russian writers Anna Akhmatova and Mikhail Zoshchenko when World War II ended.

Zweig, Stefan (1881–1942). Austrian biographer, novelist, short-story writer, and critic. Became a British citizen in 1940. Committed suicide, together with his wife, in Petropolis, Brazil.

Notes on Contributors

Horst Bienek was born in 1930 in Gleiwitz, Silesia (now Poland). In 1946 he moved to the Russian-occupied zone. Trained as a newspaper editor, he studied with Bertolt Brecht in East Berlin's "Berlin Ensemble." In 1951 Bienek was arrested for political reasons and sentenced to twenty-five years of hard labor.

Deported to Vorkuta, Siberia (in the Gulag Archipelago), he worked in a coal mine for four years. In 1955 he was granted amnesty. Since 1956 he has lived in West Germany, working first as a radio editor and then as editor-in-chief of Germany's largest pocket book publisher. Currently he is an author living in Munich.

Bienek achieved recognition through his books *Traumbuch eines Gefangenen* (1957), *Die Zelle* (1968), *Bakunin, eine Invention* (1970), and, especially, a fictional tetralogy describing his childhood during the war: *The First Polka* (1975), *September Light* (1977), *Time Without Bells* (1979), and *Earth and Fire* (1982). His books have been translated into twelve languages.

Bienek has also worked as a filmmaker. His cinematic work includes the last documentary on Ezra Pound (1966), which was purchased by the Museum of Modern Art in New York. *Die Zelle*, based on his book of the same title, was awarded first prize at the Film Festival for Human Rights in Strasbourg, France, in 1972. Bienek has received numerous literary prizes, including the Bremer Prize for Literature, the Wilhelm-Raabe Prize, the Nelly Sachs Prize, and the Prize for Historical Literary Writing. He is currently vice president of the Bavarian Academy of Fine Arts in Munich.

Joseph Brodsky was born in Leningrad in 1940. He began writing poetry when he was eighteen years old. Anna Akhmatova soon recognized the young poet as one of the most gifted voices of his generation. From March 1964 until November 1965 Brodsky lived in exile in the Arkhangelsk region of northern Russia, sentenced to five years of hard labor for "social parasitism." He did not serve out the full term.

Four of Brodsky's poems were published in Leningrad anthologies in 1966 and 1967, and the Soviet journal *Novy mir* published a selection of his verse in 1987. However, the majority of his work has appeared only in the West. He has translated the English metaphysical poets and the Polish émigré Czesław Miłosz into Russian. His own poems have been translated into at least eight languages. Among his works published in English are *Joseph Brodsky: Selected Poems* (1973), *A Part of Speech* (1980), and *Less than One* (1986), a collection of essays which won the Book Critics Circle Award.

On June 4, 1972, Brodsky became an involuntary exile from his native land. After brief stays in Vienna and London, he came to the United States. He has been poet in residence and visiting professor at the University of Michigan, Queens College, Smith College, Columbia University, and Cambridge University in England. He is affiliated with New York University and the University of Michigan, and is Five-College Professor of Literature at Mount Holyoke College.

In 1978 Brodsky was awarded the honorary degree of Doctor of Letters at Yale University. In May 1979 he was inducted as a member of the American Academy and Institute of Arts and Letters. In 1981 he received a John D. and Catherine T. MacArthur Foundation Award for his "works of genius." In October 1987, he was awarded the Nobel Prize.

To Urania, his first collection of poems since *A Part of Speech*, appeared in 1988.

Dennis Brutus was born in 1924 in Harare, Zimbabwe (then Salisbury, Rhodesia). Much of his poetry centers on his suffering and that of his fellow blacks in South Africa.

Brutus taught English and Afrikaans in South Africa for many years. Because of his outspoken protests against apartheid in sports, he received a prison sentence and was banned from teaching, writing, publishing, attending social or political meetings, and pursuing his studies in law at the University of Witwatersrand.

After leaving South Africa in 1966, Brutus worked in England and then taught at the University of Denver in the United States. In 1971 he became professor of African literature at Northwestern University. Brutus was largely responsible for South Africa's exclusion from the Olympic Games for practicing racial segregation throughout its school athletics. In the late 1960s he served as director of the World Campaign for the Release of South African Prisoners. At present he is head of the Department of Black Community Education Research and Development at the University of Pittsburgh and professor of African literature.

Brutus's published works include *Letters to Martha and Other Poems from a South African Prison* (1968), *A Simple Lust* (1973), *Stubborn Hope* (1978), and *Salutes and Censures* (1982).

Guillermo Cabrera Infante was born in 1929 in Gibara, Cuba. He received his baccalaureate in 1948 and graduated from the School of Journalism in 1956.

In 1954 Cabrera Infante became a film critic for the popular magazine *Carteles*. In 1957 he became managing editor, a position he held until the magazine was closed down. From its inception in 1959 he was the editor-in-chief of *Lunes*, a supplement to the newspaper *Revolucion*. It was banned by the government in 1961.

In 1962 Cabrera Infante was sent to Brussels as cultural attaché at the embassy; in 1964 he was promoted to chargé d'affaires. In 1965 he returned to Havana for his mother's funeral and was forcibly detained for three months. After this experience he managed to leave the country for good, moving first to Madrid and then, under pressure from Franco's government, to London.

His works include *Three Trapped Tigers* (1971); *View of Dawn in the Tropics* (1978); *Infante's Inferno* (1984); and his first book written in English, *Holy Smoke* (1985). He has also written screenplays under the pseudonym Guillermo Cain. These include *Wonderwall* (1968); *Vanishing Point* (1970); and a film adaptation of Malcolm Lowry's *Under the Volcano*, commissioned by the late film director Joseph Losey in 1972 and soon to be published as an independent work.

Cabrera Infante has also worked as a translator. Among his translations into Spanish are stories by Mark Twain, Ambrose Bierce, Sherwood Anderson, Ernest Hemingway, William Faulkner, Dashiell Hammett, J. D. Salinger, Vladimir Nabokov, and James Joyce. He has been a contributor to *The New Yorker* and *The New Republic*, as well as to Latin American and Spanish periodicals.

His honors include the Biblioteca Breve Prize for fiction (1964), the Prix du Meilleur Livre Etranger (1971), and a Guggenheim Fellowship for creative writing (1970). He has just completed a book of political essays entitled *Mea Cuba* and is working on a new novel, *Ithaca Revisited*.

Sergei Dovlatov was born in Ufa, Bashkiria (USSR). He grew up in Leningrad, enrolled in the University of Leningrad, and in 1962 was expelled for contacts with foreigners. He was then drafted into the army to serve as a guard in a forced-labor camp. These events influenced him greatly and served as a catalyst in his literary career.

In the mid-1960s Dovlatov returned to Leningrad and wrote continually. No Soviet official magazine would publish his stories, but his writings spread illegally underground. In the early 1970s they reached the West and were published by several Russian-language magazines. As a result he was persecuted, losing all work, and was finally forced to leave with his family for the United States.

In America he published several books in Russian and in English translation. His novels reflect the evolving phases of his life experience: *Invisible Book*, about the life of young literary bohemians; *The Zone*, about the horror of labor camps; *Our People*, about family ties; and *Foreigner Girl*, about the everyday ordeals of Soviet immigrants in New York. Several of his stories have appeared in *The New Yorker*.

The theme of Dovlatov's writing, if a main theme can be established, is that the absurd becomes an acceptable norm under certain conditions, while the normal becomes surprising.

Yuri Druzhnikov was born in 1923 and worked in the USSR as a journalist, teacher, and writer. He published both prose and poetry in the USSR, and some of his work circulated in *samizdat*. After applying for permission to emigrate in 1977, he published several short prose pieces in the Russian émigré journal *Time and We*, which first appeared in Israel before moving operations to the United States. Mr. Druzhnikov was finally permitted to emigrate in 1987.

Jorge Edwards was born in Santiago, Chile, in 1931. He studied law and philosophy at the University of Chile and public and international affairs at Princeton University in the United States. From 1957 to 1973 he was a diplomat in France, Peru and Cuba.

In October 1973 Edwards ended his diplomatic career by publishing an article in *Le monde* about the Chilean military coup. From 1973 to 1978 he lived in Barcelona, where he worked with the publishing house Seix Barral and wrote for the Spanish press. He returned to Chile in 1978, where, in 1980, he became the head of the Committee for Freedom of Expression, created by the Society of Chilean Writers and by journalists' associations. He served for three years. Presently he is a member of the Committee for Free Elections.

Jorge Edwards's first book of short stories, *El patio*, was published in 1952. Today his short stories and novels are widely read in Spain and Latin America and have been translated into French. His works are currently being translated into several other European languages.

Edwards's principal books are *El peso de la noche* (1964), *Los convidados de piedra* (1978), *El museo de cera* (1981), *La mujer imaginaria* (1985), and *El anfitrión*, which will soon be published in Spain and in Latin America. He is also known for his nonfiction work *Persona non grata* (1974), which created a political and literary scandal in Spain, France, and Latin America. Its publication marked the first time a leftist Latin American writer sharply criticized Castro's Cuba, giving an inside account of relations between dissident Cuban writers and the state. The book, a day-by-day account of Edwards's diplomacy for Allende's socialist government in Havana from December 1970 to April 1971, has also been published in England and Italy.

Nuruddin Farah was born in 1945 in Baidoa, Somalia. He worked in the Ministry of Education before leaving for India to study philosophy and literature at the University of Chaudigarh.

Farah has traveled widely in Africa, Europe, and North America and speaks five languages. He has taught at the University of Mogadiscio as well as the universities of London, Essex, and Bayreuth, where he was guest professor in the Department of Comparative Literature.

His novels include *From a Crooked Rib* (1970); *A Naked Needle* (1976); the trilogy *Sweet & Sour Milk* (1979), *Sardines* (1981), and *Close Sesame* (1983); and most recently *Maps* (1986), which, like his previous work, is a novel about modern Africa and the anguish of living on a continent where national boundaries have been drawn by foreign hands.

William Gass was born in Fargo, North Dakota, in 1924. He received his B.A. from Kenyon College and his Ph.D. from Cornell University. He has been professor of philosophy at Purdue University and the University of Illinois. Since 1980 he has been Distinguished University Professor in the Humanities at Washington University, St. Louis.

Gass is the author of *Omensetter's Luck* (1966), *In the Heart of the Heart of the Country and Other Stories* (1968), *Willie Master's Lonesome Wife* (1968), *Fiction and the Figures of Life* (1970), *On Being Blue* (1976), *The World Within the Word* (1978), and *The Habitations of the Word* (1984), which won the Book Critics Circle Award for Criticism.

He is a member of the Academy and Institute of Arts and Letters and the American Academy of Arts and Sciences. Gass is currently at work on three projects: a novel entitled *The Tunnel*; a collection entitled *Four Essays on Architecture*; and *The Surface of the City*, a book of essays he has written to accompany his photographs.

John Glad holds a Ph.D. in Slavic literatures from New York University and is a professor of Russian literature at the University of Maryland. He is the former director of the Kennan Institute for Advanced Russian Studies in the Woodrow Wilson International Center for Scholars in Washington, D.C.

The author of numerous scholarly publications, including a book on Russian phonetics, Glad has translated books, articles, and verse on the topic of human rights. Among his translations are *The Black Book* (with James Levine, 1981), about German concentration camps; Varlam Shalamov's short stories *Kolyma Tales* (1980) and *Graphite* (1981), about the Soviet forced-labor camps; and *Soviet Dissident Movements* (with Carol Pearce, 1985).

Glad has published and translated widely in the area of Russian literature in exile. His work includes nineteen articles on Russian émigré writers in the *Yale Handbook on Russian Literature*. He has also coedited, with Daniel Weissbort, *Russian Poetry: The Modern Period* (1978).

Glad's awards for scholarship and translation include a Guggenheim Fellowship, the Olin Senior Research Award, and fellowships from the National Endowment for Humanities and the National Endowment for Democracy. Both his translations of *Kolyma Tales* and *Russian Poetry: The Modern Period* have been "Recommended Choices" of the book editor of the *New York Times*. *Kolyma Tales* was selected as one of the five best translations of the year in the 1980 American Book Awards. In addition, Glad's edition and translation of the verse of the Russian poet Nikolai Klyuev won the Translation Award from the Columbia University School of the Arts.

Currently Glad is writing a history of Russian literature in exile, which will be accompanied by a second volume of interviews with Russian writers in exile. *Literature in Exile* is Glad's third collaboration with style editor Susan Ashe. Their first two collaborations were *Kolyma Tales* and *Graphite*.

Jiří Gruša was born in Pardubice, Czechoslovakia, in 1938. He received a degree from Charles University in Prague in 1962.

He was the founder of the literary magazine *Tvar* in 1964, a member of the editorial staff of the magazine *Knižní noviny* beginning in 1967, a cofounder of the literary magazine *Sešity* in 1967, and a member of the editorial staff of *Zitrek* beginning in 1968. He became associated with the Prague Theater, "Behind the Gate," in 1972. From the start of his career as a writer, Gruša was in conflict with the authorities; as a result he was periodically unemployed and his work suppressed.

In 1978 he was arrested for "the crime of initiating disorder." At issue was his novel *The Questionnaire* (1974), which supposedly "contained grave calumnies against socialism and the Czech political system." Gruša's arrest attracted world attention, and as a result of protests he was released after two months. However, it was a year before the charges were dropped. In 1980 Gruša was exiled from Czechoslovakia. He was stripped of Czech citizenship in 1981. He has settled in West Germany.

Gruša's other written work includes the poetry collections *The Knapsack* (1962), *The Bright Days of Grace* (1964), *Practicing Torture* (1969), and *Prayer to Jeanet* (1974); the novel *Mimner; or, How to Play the Stinker* (1974); children's literature; and short stories. He has edited various collections and contributed to periodicals, including *Kontinent*, *Svĕdectvi*, and *Sešity*. In 1983 he published his first work written in Germany, *Franz Kafka of Prague*.

Nedim Gürsel was born in 1951 in southeastern Turkey. He began his literary career writing short stories, which were published in various literary magazines.

He studied in Paris, where in 1979 he earned a Ph.D. in French literature under the direction of Etiemble. He wrote his thesis on the work of Aragon and Nâzim Hikmet. His first novel, *Un long été à Istanbul*, was published in France by Gallimard in 1980 and obtained the highest literary distinction in Turkey. This novel was translated into several foreign languages. In addition, Gürsel has published a collection of short stories, *Les lapins du commandant*, numerous critical essays, and an important study of the poetry of Nâzim Hikmet. His novel *La première femme*, which appeared recently in Turkey, was seized by the Turkish authorities for "offending public morals."

At present Gürsel lives in Paris, where he directs research at the Centre National des Recherches Scientifiques and teaches at the Sorbonne.

Wojciech Karpinski was born in Poland in 1943. He studied Romance literatures and philosophy at Warsaw University, receiving his M.A. in 1966 and his Ph.D. in 1970. That same year he was expelled from the university for political reasons. During the 1970s he was active in independent cultural movements in Poland. He coedited *Res publica*, an underground quarterly, and was a contributor to *Tygodnik powszechny*, the leading Catholic weekly. He was also on the staff of the literary monthly *Twórczość*. Always interested in the work of Polish exiles, Karpinski wrote about such work in the official as well as the underground press.

In the fall of 1981 Karpinski was invited to the United States. He was there during the coup d'état against *Solidarity*; his name was on the official list of people being interned in Poland. In exile, he taught at Yale University for one semester. Then, in the fall of 1982, he entered the Centre National de la Recherche Scientifique, which is affiliated with the École des Hautes Études en Sciences Sociales in Paris. He is now also a member of the editorial board of *Zeszyty literackie*, a Polish literary quarterly published in Paris.

Karpinski's essays concern the history of ideas, art criticism, and literary criticism. His published work includes *Modern French Criticism* (1974), *In Central Park* (1982), *American Shadows* (1983), and *Metternich's Shadow* (1983). He is currently completing a book on Polish writers in exile.

Karpinski has been the recipient of the Kościelski Foundation Award (Geneva,

1975), the Ingram Merrill Award (New York, 1977), and the Award of the Union of Polish Writers Abroad (London, 1984).

Richard E. Kim was born in 1932 in Hamheung, North Korea. He served in the Republic of Korea (South) Mariens and Army from 1950 to 1954, was honorably discharged as first lieutenant, infantry, and came to the United States in 1954.

Kim was educated at Middlebury College, where he studied political science and history from 1955 to 1959, at Johns Hopkins University (M.A., writing, 1960), at the University of Iowa Writers' Workshop (M.F.A., 1962), and at Harvard University (M.A., Far Eastern languages and literature, 1963).

His academic experience includes various professorships in English at the University of Massachusetts at Amherst, Syracuse University, San Diego State University, and at Seoul National University, where he was a Fulbright Professor from 1981 to 1983.

Kim's published original works include *In Search of Lost Years* (1985), *A Blue Bird (A Children's Story)* (1983), *Lost Names* (1970), *The Innocent* (1968), and *The Martyred* (1964). He has translated into Korean a number of works, including *More Die of Heartbreak*, by Saul Bellow (1987); *The Garden of Eden*, by Ernest Hemingway (1986); and *The Ascent of Man*, by J. Bronowski (1985). He has also written for South Korean television.

Among his awards and honors are the National Endowment for the Arts Literary Fellowship (1978–79); the first award, Modern Korean Literature Translation Awards (1974); a Guggenheim Fellowship (1966); and a Ford Foundation Foreign Area Fellowship (1962–63).

Lev Kopelev was born in Kiev in 1912. He studied at Kharkov State University, the Moscow Institute of Foreign Languages, and the Moscow Institute of Philosophy, History, and Literature.

Writer, critic, and historian, Kopelev is best known in the West for his three volumes of memoirs and for his dissident activities. Although inspired by Communism as a youth, Kopelev was arrested for his un-Soviet attitudes in 1945 and imprisoned for ten years. After his release, he continued to protest against Soviet repression. His human rights activities resulted in expulsion from the Communist Party in 1968 and from the Soviet Writers' Union in 1977. Throughout, Kopelev remained committed to Russia and refused to emigrate until, in 1981, the government stripped him of his citizenship while he was visiting the West.

In addition to his memorable trilogy *To Be Preserved Forever* (1977), *The Education of a True Believer* (1980), and *Ease My Sorrows* (1983), Kopelev is known for his work in linguistics and for his extensive writings on German literature. He has translated works by Goethe, Brecht, and Böll into Russian.

At present he is editing two series of books for Wuppertal University entitled *German Literature of the Seventeenth to the Twentieth Centuries* and *Germany and the Germans in Russian Literature of the Seventeenth to the Twentieth Centuries*.

Kopelev received the Friedrich Gundolf Prize from the German Academy of Language and Poetry in 1980; the Peace Prize of the German Book Trade from the

German Booksellers Association in 1981; and the Culture Prize from the German Freemasons in 1983. He was a Visiting Fellow at Columbia University in 1981 and a visiting professor at Yale University in 1982. Kopelev was awarded honorary doctorates from Cologne University and from the New School for Social Research in 1981.

Antonin Liehm was born in 1924, in Prague, Czechoslovakia. He received a degree in political science from Charles University in 1949. In 1970 he emigrated to the United States.

Liehm has held professorships at the University of Paris (1969–1970), the City University of New York (1970–1976), the University of Pennsylvania (1977–1981), the University of Paris (1982–1987), and the École des Hautes Études en Sciences Sociales, Paris (1987). In 1976–1977 he worked as a tutor at the National Film School in London. A keen political observer, he explores in particular the relationship between politics and culture. Liehm was the organizer and coordinator of the Biennial on Dissident Culture in Eastern Europe (Venice, 1977). In 1984 he founded and became editor of the European intellectual journal *Lettre Internationale*, published in Paris, Rome, Madrid, and Berlin.

Liehm's writings include *Interview* (1964), *Politics of Culture* (1972), *Closely Watched Films* (1973), and *The Most Important Art* (1977). He was a member of the editorial board of *Literarni noviny* from 1961 to 1969.

Liehm is also a member of International PEN, the American Association for the Advancement of Slavic Studies, the Society for Cinema Studies, and the Czechoslovak Society of Arts and Sciences. He received a Guggenheim Fellowship in 1972 and the Theatre Library Award in 1978.

Edward Limonov was born in 1944 in Dzerzhinsk, USSR, the son of a military officer. He spent his childhood and adolescence in Kharkov. He wrote his first poem at the age of fifteen.

In 1967 he moved to Moscow, where he lived until emigrating to the West in 1974. He settled in New York City in 1975. In 1980 he moved to France, where he now lives.

Limonov has had a long and colorful list of occupations: thief, construction worker, mover, tailor, painter, steelworker, busboy, cook, butler, and poet. Since his first publication in France in 1980, he has worked as a professional writer.

Limonov's books include *It's Me, Eddie* (1983); and *His Butler's Story* (1987), based on his experiences working as a housekeeper for a New York City multi-millionaire. To date his work has been translated into eight languages. In addition, he has contributed to such publications as *Liberation, Playboy, Globe,* and *Le journal littéraire.*

Yury Miloslavsky was born in 1946 in Kharkov, USSR. From the age of seventeen he played an active part in the city's unofficial literary scene as a poet and author of "black humor" surrealistic texts. He received his M.A. in Russian literature from Kharkov University. Miloslavsky has held numerous and varied jobs: manual worker, streetcar ticket collector, puppet theater actor, and journalist.

Miloslavsky emigrated in 1973 and has lived in Jerusalem ever since. For a while he was editor-in-chief of a small Russian-language paper. He began writing prose relatively late in life. The first part of *Fortified Cities*, a novel describing the fortunes of Soviet immigrants in Israel, was published in 1978 and provoked bitter arguments in the press, including accusations of "anti-Zionist sentiments."

The complete text of *Fortified Cities* was published in 1980. It was followed by *Poems* (1983), and *For the Noise of Horsemen and Bowmen* (1984), a collection of short stories. Miloslavsky has also published critical essays and articles on literary history. He is the author of studies on the history of the New Testament period, feasts of the Eastern Church, and the holy places of Palestine. He is also known as a radio journalist specializing in Middle Eastern affairs.

Miloslavsky was a participant in the Continent of Culture Writers' Congress in Milan, Italy, in 1983; and in the colloquium on the New Russian Prose at Fribourg University, Switzerland, in 1987.

Libuše Moníková was born in Prague, Czechoslovakia, in 1945. She studied at Charles University in Prague, graduating with a doctoral dissertation on the Coriolanus theme in Shakespeare and Brecht. Since 1971 she has been living in West Germany. Before becoming a writer, she worked at the universities of Kassel and Bremen as a lecturer in German literature.

Moníková's published works are *Eine Schädigung* (1981), *Pavane für eine Verstorbene Infantin* (1983), and *Die Fassade* (1987). Although her native language is Czech, she writes in German. *Die Fassade*, her most recent work, spans the history of Europe from the eighteenth century to ten years after the Soviet occupation of Czechoslovakia. Her work is scheduled for translation into English, French, and Italian; translations into Greek, Dutch, Danish, Swedish, and Finnish are also forthcoming. In addition to her novels she has published several essays and plays.

Moníková has received several literary honors, including the *Ehrengabe der Deutschen Industrie* in 1984 and the 1987 Alfred Doeblin Prize, founded by Günter Grass. She was an active participant in the Berlin Encounter of Eastern and Western authors.

Jan Novak was born in Kolin, Czechoslovakia, in 1953. He and his family relocated to Chicago in 1969 following ten months in Austrian refugee camps. He was educated at the University of Chicago, where he received a B.A. and M.A. in humanities. Novak lives in Chicago and has been earning a living as a computer operations supervisor for the local phone company since 1978.

Novak's writings were originally in Czech; his first book, *Striptease Chicago*, is a collection of interconnected short stories depicting Czech émigré life in Chicago. Its frank treatment of various peculiarities of the community where men heavily outnumber women has enraged the Czech-American ghetto. He has also written several plays in his native language—*Czechs* and *The Wrong Way Out*—later translating them into English. Novak gradually began to write in English, beginning with the plays *The Sperm Count* and *Uncle Joe*, then continuing with fiction and poetry. Since 1982 he has been writing almost exclusively in English.

Novak's first novel was *The Willys Dream Kit*, a story of embezzlement and gambling in a small town in Eastern Europe and also of immigration and gambling in America. The story closely resembles that of his own family. In 1985 the work received the Sandburg Prize as the best work of Chicago fiction and was nominated for the Pulitzer Prize. *The Grand Life*, just released, was inspired by the nonsensical vernacular of computer bureaucrats.

Novak has translated into English two plays by Václav Havel, *The Audience* and *Unveiling*, which were produced by the Northlight Theatre of Chicago in 1986. He has also completed a screenplay and, more recently, finished the first draft of another novel, tentatively titled *Love on Company Time*.

Raissa Orlova-Kopelev was born in Moscow in 1918. She studied at the Moscow Institute of Philosophy, History, and Literature and at the Moscow Institute for World Literature, specializing in American literature. She married Lev Kopelev in 1958.

Known as a literary critic, memoirist, and translator, Orlova-Kopelev pursued her interest in American literature in the Soviet Union as a professor and editor, publishing books and numerous articles in the Soviet press. From the mid-sixties she was drawn into the human rights movement, gradually becoming a dissident. Her activities in defense of Soviet scientist and activist Andrei Sakharov caused her to lose her membership in the Communist Party and the Soviet Writers' Union. Along with her husband, she was stripped of Soviet citizenship in 1981.

Her works, some written with Lev Kopelev, have been featured in *Novoye russkoye slovo*, *Russkaya mysl'*, and other Russian émigré and Western publications. She died of cancer in 1989.

Anton Shammas was born in 1950 in Fassuta, Upper Galilee. He studied English literature and the history of art at the Hebrew University in Jerusalem. During the 1970s he was coeditor of the Arabic literary magazine *A-sharq*, in which he published many of his translations from modern Hebrew literature. From 1976 to 1986 he worked for Israeli TV as a producer of Arabic programs. In recent years he has written a weekly column for two newspapers, *Kol-ha'eer* of Jerusalem and *Ha'eer* of Tel Aviv.

Shammas writes in both Arabic and Hebrew. His first novel, *Arabesques* (1986), originally published in Hebrew, will be released in English and in several European languages in 1988. His other publications include the volumes of poetry *Poems* (Arabic, 1974) and *No Man's Land* (Hebrew, 1979); and a children's book, *The Biggest Liar in the World* (1982). His translations include works by Samuel Beckett, Athol Fugard, and Emile Habibi.

Shammas received the Prime Minister's Award for Creative Writing, 1980–1981. He is currently writer in residence at the Center for Near Eastern Studies at the University of Michigan as a Rockefeller Fellow in Middle Eastern Literature.

Virgil Tanase was born in Rumania in 1945. He studied literature and scenography and received a doctorate under the supervision of Roland Barthes. After his books were banned from publication in Rumania and a play he was directing was suppressed, Tanase established himself in France in 1977. There he published six novels: *Portrait d'homme à la faux dans un paysage marin* (1976), *Apocalypse d'un adolescent de* *bonne famille* (1980), *L'amour, l'amour, roman sentimental* (1982), *Cette morte qui va et vient et revient* (1984), *Le bal sur la goelette du pirate aveugle* (1987), and *Le bal autour du diamant magique* (1987). In 1982 he staged his play *Le paradis à l'amiable* at the Théâtre Lucenaire in Paris.

Tanase is now a French citizen and writes in French. He also works as a translator, stage director, and journalist. He is an *Officier des Arts et des Lettres.*

Jaroslav Vejvoda was born in Prague, Czechoslovakia, in 1940. He received his M.A. in law from Charles University in 1962. From 1962 until 1968 he worked in Prague as a lawyer and journalist. In 1968 he left Czechoslovakia for Switzerland, where he has been working as a lecturer and writer.

Vejvoda's work includes collections of short stories, *Floating Angels, Flying Fish* (1974) and *Birds* (1981); and the novels *The Donkey or the Bleeding* (1977) and *Green Wine* (1986).

In 1981 his collected short stories were published in West Germany under the title *Wohltätigkeitsbasar*. Two years later the book was awarded the Literary Prize of the City of Zurich, the first time a foreign author received this distinction. *Floating Angels, Flying Fish* was also awarded the Egon Hostovsky Memorial Award (New York, 1974).

The recurring theme in Vejvoda's work is the fate of immigrants, particularly of refugees in Switzerland and Western Europe. Since 1983 Vejvoda has been writing screenplays, for which he has received recognition at various festivals.

Tomas Venclova was born in 1937 in Klaipeda, Lithuania. He was the son of a prominent figure in the Lithuanian Communist party. In 1960 he received his degree in philology from Vilnius University, Lithuania. He then worked at Tartu University, Estonia. In 1985 he completed his Ph.D. at Yale University.

Venclova has had an active career as teacher, author, and translator. He taught literature and semiotics at Vilnius University and published approximately twenty papers on literary and cultural topics. He has translated works of Pasternak, Akhmatova, T. S. Eliot, Khlebnikov, Norwid, Alfred Jarry, and Mandelstam into Lithuanian. In 1972 he published a book of poems in Lithuanian, *Sign of Speech.*

While in Lithuania, Venclova became active in the dissident movement. In 1976, with the help of Yury Orlov, Alexander Ginzburg, and Anatoly Scharansky, he took part in the founding of the Lithuanian Helsinki Group.

In 1977 he left the Soviet Union to teach at the University of California at Berkeley. Because of his dissident activities, he was stripped of his Soviet citizenship. Since 1980 he has been teaching Russian literature and Lithuanian language at Yale University.

In the United States, Venclova has published two books of poetry, two books of essays, and a number of papers. He contributes to *Poetry* (Chicago), *Encounter, World Literature Today, The New Republic, The New Leader,* and *The New York Review of Books.*

He has been awarded fellowships from the New York Institute for the Humanities (1981–1984) and the Kennan Institute for Advanced Russian Studies (1981). He is a member of International PEN and is on the executive board of PEN in Exile. In addition, he is on the editorial boards of *Forum balticum* (Stockholm), *Sintaksis* (Paris), *Zeszyty literackie* (Paris), *Metmenys* (Chicago), and *Akiraciai* (Chicago).

Georgy Vladimov was born in Kharkov, Ukraine, in 1931. He graduated from a military academy in 1948 and from the Department of Law of Leningrad University in 1953.

In 1954 he began working on a provincial paper. He also published some critical articles in magazines including *Teatr*, *Novy mir* and *Literaturnaya gazeta*. From 1956 to 1959 he worked at *Novy mir* as an editor. In 1961 his first story, "The Large Ore," was published in *Novy mir*, an event which forced him to take his writings to the West. He also smuggled out to the West the novel *Faithful Ruslan* (1975), the play *The Sixth Maestro* (1981), and the short story "Don't Pay Attention, Maestro" (1982). Almost all his works have been translated into other languages. In some countries they have been published in several editions.

In 1977 Vladimov resigned from the Soviet Writers' Union in protest at the persecution of his colleagues. He joined the Moscow Group of Amnesty International and was elected chairman. The KGB continued to harass him because of his dissident activities, and in May 1983 he was forced to emigrate from the USSR to West Germany. A month later he was stripped of Soviet citizenship.

Vladimov is currently working on a novel about World War II entitled *The General and His Army*. The first chapters of this novel were published in two Russian magazines, *Kontinent* and *Grani*.

Jan Vladislav was born in 1923 in Hlohovec, Czechoslovakia. He studied foreign languages and comparative literature at the University of Grenoble in France, and at Charles University in Prague, from which he was expelled after the 1948 coup d'état. It was not until 1969 that he was able to complete his studies and to receive his Ph.D. from Charles University.

Between 1945 and 1948 Vladislav published three books of poetry and contributed critical essays, mostly about Western European literature, to various journals. He was expelled from the university for propagating decadent Western culture. After 1948 he was prevented from publishing any of his works. As a result, he devoted himself to translation, chiefly poetry, including classics such as Dante and Shakespeare. His main interest, however, was the poetry of modern Europe. As the political situation permitted, he published translations of poems by Ungaretti, Machado, Reverdy, and others. In addition, he translated and introduced the complete critical works of Baudelaire.

At the end of the 1960s several of his translations and essays were awarded Czech literary prizes. He also wrote a series of prize-winning books for children.

In 1968–1969 a number of his new works were ready for publication, including poetry, *Soliloquies* and *Sentences*; and essays, *Portraits and Self-Portraits*. However, after the 1968 occupation, their publication was forcibly halted. They were issued in the 1970s in *samizdat* before being printed by exile publishing houses after 1980. Still awaiting publication is *Open Diary 1977–1981*.

Vladislav is responsible for founding and running the *samizdat* book series

KVART (Quarto), in which he published over a hundred different titles of poetry, essays, and novels. He was one of the first signatories of Charter 77. In 1981 he was stripped of Czech citizenship and was forced to emigrate to France. He currently lectures on Central and Eastern European unofficial culture at the École des Hautes Études en Sciences Sociales in Paris, and is a member of the editorial board of the journal *L'autre Europe*.

Vladimir Voinovich was born in Tadzhikistan, USSR, in 1932. In his youth he held a variety of jobs, including herdsman on a collective farm, factory hand, and aircraft mechanic, and eventually served in the army. He moved to Moscow to study history at the Moscow Pedagogical Institute, and became a writer in 1956. In 1962 he became a member of the Union of Soviet Writers.

Voinovich enjoyed great professional success during his early years. His stories were published in *Novy mir*, his plays were widely produced, and his poems, which were set to music, became popular songs throughout much of the Soviet Union.

In 1966, two years after Khrushchev's ouster, Voinovich began taking an active role in the human-rights movement, at which time his troubles with the authorities began. Eventually the Writers' Union cut off his royalties. Forced to submit his work to Soviet publications under assumed names, Voinovich also sent his manuscripts to Western publishers. It was the appearance of *The Life and Extraordinary Adventures of Private Ivan Chonkin* in Paris, and his outspoken defense of many people, including Nobel Prize winner Aleksandr Solzhenitsyn, that resulted in Voinovich's expulsion from the Writers' Union in 1974.

Living under the constant threat of arrest for "parasitism" and increased psychological harassment by the KGB, Voinovich left the Soviet Union in December 1980 with his wife and daughter. They settled in Germany at the invitation of the Bavarian Academy of Arts. In 1981 Brezhnev officially stripped Voinovich of his Soviet citizenship.

From 1982 to 1983 Voinovich taught Russian literature at Princeton University. He is currently a member of the French division of PEN, the Mark Twain Society, the World Literary Academy, and is a contributor to a variety of publications. Voinovich's works published in the West include *The Ivankiad* (1976), *In Plain Russian* (1979), and *Pretender to the Throne* (1979).

In 1986 *The Anti-Soviet Soviet Union*, Voinovich's first book written and published after his exile, was released. *Moscow—2042* (1987) is the satirist's first novel written in the West.

Adam Zagajewski was born in 1945 in Lvov in the Polish Ukraine, now part of the USSR. He studied philosophy at Krakow University before settling in Paris in 1983.

Only a few of Zagajewski's works have been published in Poland: four volumes of poetry, two of which were published by underground presses; two novels; and two collections of literary criticism, including *The Unrepresented World*, which he co-authored. A collection of his poems, *News Every Hour: The Poems of Ten Years*, was published in West Germany in 1984. In 1987 selections of his poetry appeared in Sweden and in Norway. His novel *The Thin Line* was published in West Germany

(1985) and in France (1987); *Solidarity and Solitude,* a collection of essays, appeared in both countries in 1986. His essays have been published in Hebrew, Italian, German, and Greek.

Tremor: Collected Poems was the first collection of Zagajewski's poetry to appear in English.

Library of Congress Cataloging-in-Publication Data

Literature in exile / edited by John Glad

Based on a conference held on Dec. 2–5, 1987 in Vienna and

organized by staff of the Wheatland Foundation.

ISBN 0-8223-0987-4

1. Literature—Exiled authors—History and criticism. 2. Authors, Exiled.

3. Literature, Modern—20th century—History and criticism. 4. Politics and

literature. I. Glad, John. II. Wheatland Foundation.

PN495.P47 1990   809'.8920694—dc20   89-39904 CIP